DOCENT
DETAILS

REFLECTIONS ON DOCENT
LIFE IN ART MUSEUMS

By Ivy Hendy

Illustrations by Paul Lee

Photographs by Jeff Hendy

Printed in the United States of America

I Street Press
828 I Street
Sacramento, CA 95814

Hendy, Ivy
     Docent Details:
     Reflections on Docent Life in Art Museums
     by Ivy Hendy
     Illustrations by Paul Lee
     Photos by Jeff Hendy

     p. cm.
     ISBN: 978-0-9889839-0-8

     1.   Travel/ Museums, Tours, Points of Interest
     2.   Business & Economics/ Museum Administration
        & Museology
     LCCN: 20136 908 185

Cover Photo of Museum of Modern Art, NY,
Photographed and Designed by Jeff Hendy

This book is dedicated to the thousands of art docents who selflessly work to enhance and enrich the knowledge and pleasure of the museum-going public.

Contents

Acknowledgments

Among the many people to whom I am indebted for help in the preparation of this book, I must single out my illustrator, Paul Lee for his brilliant assistance in creating the professional sketches which make my stories come to life in a delightful, visual way; Don Zinter for his careful reading and wise suggestions; Scott O'Connor for generously contributing his essay regarding male docents; and above all, my husband, Jeff, for his endless help and support.

To these people and the many others whose encouraging words braced me in the days when it was difficult to sit down at the computer, I send my heartfelt and grateful thanks.

Preface

Docent Details: My Own Journey

The artwork is spectacular, I thought, the first time I walked through the Museum of Modern Art in San Francisco. This experience sent me on the most significant journey of my life. Upon leaving the museum premises, the cosmopolitan skyline became a mixture of lines and brush strokes. Narrow strands of tall grass became frail bones jutting up from the soil. The curve of a human spine, the dark hue of chocolate pudding, the scratchy flow of an ink pen on paper…my world became vivid and alive. Through the years, the inspiration I have acquired from museums has allowed me to build a cognitive framework to make more sense of my life.

Luckily for me the museums always offered voluntary tours. This was particularly helpful for me in the beginning because I was a person who was working with only a thread of understanding of the artworks. The first tour I joined was when I visited the Metropolitan Museum of Art in New York City. The tour guide showed our group around that venerable institution in a manner that made the artworks come to life. He seemed to be able to do it with the flip of his tongue, a sleight of hand and perhaps a casting of spells. With hindsight I now see that good tour guides have a veritable suitcase of talents;

3

when not discussing facts, they call on other strategies like storytelling. To me it was magic.

In foreign countries I have been amazed at tour guides in art museums who, because of their restricted knowledge of English or their heavy accents, are still able to illuminate the works for someone like myself. It is a seeming contradiction that a tour guide can impart awareness to a foreigner when, in fact, nothing that is said is in a comprehensible language. What I must have heard was the tone of the voice, the admiration of the aesthetic, and the recognition of the appealing. I will be forever indebted to all those docents, both those in my country and those who are located abroad, who work so hard to give us glimpses of what they themselves already know.

The consequence of all this was that I found myself more and more wanting to visit art museums for a "fix," just as a person would who is unalterably addicted. I have an insatiable interest in seeing the artistic creations of others. I can acknowledge this because at least my form of dependency is legal, and not in any particular need of intervention. Nor is being an art lover a lonely affair; happily, we are not the only children of a lost species.

The muse of creativity visited me at an early age and I have been producing art in the form of sketches, paintings and sculptures since I was a child. In the past I sat on museum floors sketching the works of masters. Though I now still dabble at artistic works, in my creative endeavors I follow Picasso's guiding principle: "Good artists copy. Great artists steal." But to avoid embarrassment, for the most part the viewers of my art are restricted to the ubiquitous dust mites.

In searching out museums, my pastime has taken me to many areas of the world. I have crawled through cave tunnels in Spain to be awed by authentic Neolithic art. The indigenous art in the Australian museums has been particularly moving for me, as has the primitive art in Tanzania. I have visited many of the famous and adored museums in Europe and North America. There are many museum which, for me, are unforgettable: the Beijing Museum, the "gold" museum in Lima, the National Museum of Anthropology in Mexico City: even though some museums are considered historical, archeological or anthropological, they hold the artistic objects of the past disguised as such things as functional items or religious icons.

I have been lucky to have had opportunities to visit impressive places and seen remarkable collections not because of a lofty social status nor, regretfully, because of a well-heeled family fortune, but because I felt a tug at the heart to see as much of the artworks of mankind as possible.

I have found that being a docent in an art museum also requires a journey; one of the mind. It is a soothing site where the voices of many muses are visibly transferred. And one is never too young or too old to become a tour guide in an art museum. I was in my early thirties when I was a docent at the San Francisco Museum of Modern Art. In recent years docent work has kept me occupied at the Crocker Art Museum in Sacramento.

I give you this book as the result of my wanderings and musings, a gift for those of you who are on the quest for a meaningful life-long activity that includes artistic creations.

One prerequisite for art docent work is that you enjoy sharing your love of art with others; another is that you keep to a position of neutrality. There will inevitably be some works that will hold claim on your heart and mind. Your love can't reveal itself as a bias. There have been times when I have found this requirement a difficult obligation to keep. But when I remember its fundamental truth, I have found that within the kernel of the thing lurks the possibility for fair-mindedness.

If you are thinking of pursuing the world of tour guide in an art museum, you have picked the right book.

I'll see you at the museum.

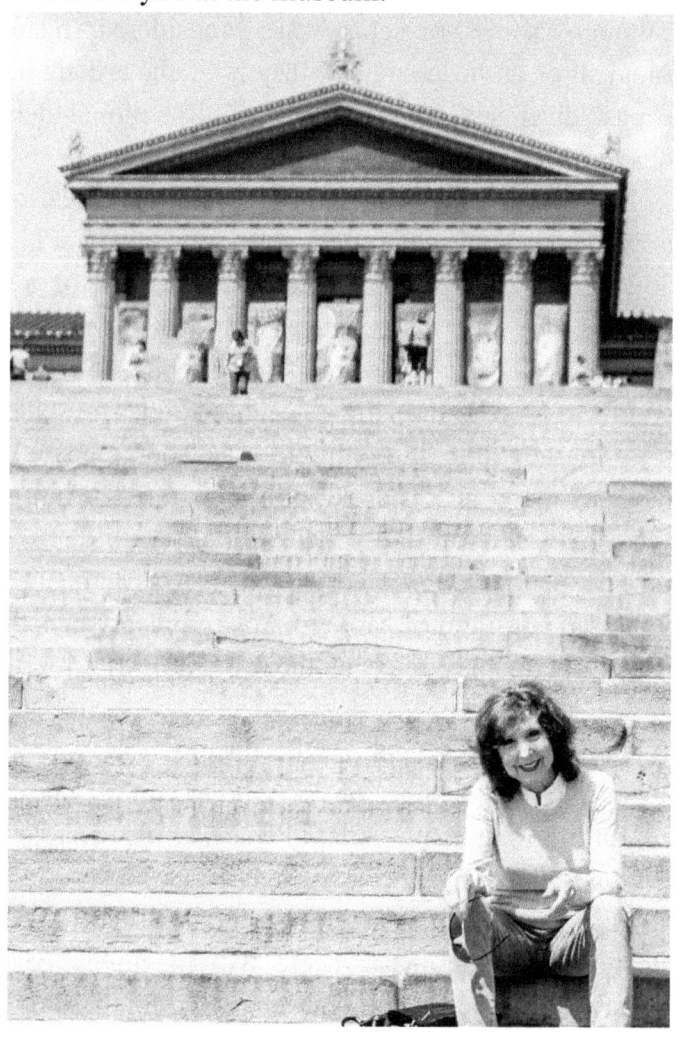

On the steps of the Philadelphia Museum of Art

Introduction: Painting the Picture

"What do docents do? "
"But of course, they explain the endeavors of others."
Michael Cary, artist/philosopher

Art museums have great art collections. They also have curious visitors. The best way to connect the art collections to the visitors is with a good docent tour. Some museums have collections that are more self-explanatory than others. To give a comparison: in a natural science museum featuring an exhibit of dinosaur bones, tours are probably less needed. The dinosaurs left large, gnarled skeletons which can be dramatic, scary and capable of being exhibited without more than a few terse scientific words on the signage.

Artworks produced by humans do not compare in theatricality to these prehistoric creatures' remains. Nor are human works as immediately comprehensible as a large T-Rex skeleton. Instead, the works of art are reflections of the human mind, and the human mind, as we all know, can be complex, ambiguous and conflicted.

Just looking at art works of the past, whether eons or decades old requires some interpretation. The items were painted, drawn, carved, or forged for an entirely different audience. Even a fifty year old "contemporary" art piece was created for a group of spectators who no longer exist. Time and space, as Einstein pointed out, are relative. What was *de rigueur* in the popular tastes of yesterday might be difficult to comprehend today. This obvious conundrum poses a problem for any museum of art: how to bring visitors into the narrative of an art piece and form a bond?

There are those who would argue that a work of art is a work of creativity which stands alone through time, with no necessity for subtext or descriptive comment. Though true on one level, this argument misses some of the subtleties of appealing to current preferences. As time goes by, art which originally was clear has become much more mystifying as meanings, symbols, fashion and intent change. It is easy for a casual visitor to walk past a work which at first looks too different or impenetrable to understand. But pointing out art works that are not the normal fare can cause a museum visitor to look more closely. The responsibility of bringing an active visual experience and understanding to a museum guest is the job of the **art museum docent**.

You are about to enter the world of art docents---a world where the obscure can be made obvious and a love of art prevails. Yet, a lot is riding on each individual docent. Here is the docent definition: a docent is a tour guide; a docent is a person who can cause a museum visitor to look more closely at art; a docent is a person who brings art works to life by selectively suggesting ways to look at an art piece, thereby bringing a new awareness to a museum visitor; docent is a gate keeper; a docent is a person who volunteers hours of time equity for the recompense of a smile.

There is much that is noble in the intent of a docent; yet it is a job which weighs heavily. This book takes a candid, non-technical and lighthearted look at what the world of the art docent consists of; its triumphs and its foibles. At times the stories may seem exaggerated: in reality there is no way to make up the many heart-rending, unusual and sometimes baffling happenings of docent experiences. As each docent is an individual, so each visitor to a museum is as well. And though docents have been trained by the museum, no such museum etiquette has been taught to the general public who have various and sundry reactions to the works on a tour. Their reactions can range from flummoxed, to delighted to bizarre responses so unique that they stretch the realm of credulity.

Included in this book are a myriad of tips and techniques for the person who is thinking of becoming a docent or is an experienced docent and wants a few fresh and light-hearted thoughts on touring. Finally, there are docent details in this book that you will find nowhere else; frank discussions of subjects not usually discussed. The world of docents, just like the real world, exists in a stasis between ambiguity and clarity---sometimes both existing at the same time. No attempt has been made to tint the pigments or change the palette. The painted picture of the docent world unfolds here: it is for you, dear reader, to judge the tour. I hope you will follow me up the stairs of the museum as we get started. Come along…..

Chapter One

Beginnings of Art and Art Institutions

The Urge to Create

A hundred thousand years ago, when *Homo sapiens* were in their early development, an artisan sat in a cave in what is now part of South Africa and using a pestle, crushed material into a small abalone shell. The material was a blend of yellow ochre, marrow from animal bones, charcoal from a fire pit, and water. This now dried and dusty primitive blend, still extant today in its mortar and with its pestle, is the first evidence we have that humans purposefully mixed paint. Though the cave walls in South Africa where the dried paint matter is located are covered with thousands of years of encrusted limestone and do not reveal their secrets, the mixture was undoubtedly used for decorating either the enclosing space of the cave or the humans themselves; perhaps both. The cave is Blombos and sits on a cliff 180 miles east of Cape Town. The primitive paint tool kit reflects the deep roots of the impulse for humans to create some form of art.

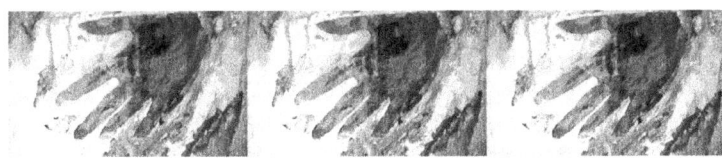

Paintings on the Walls

The earliest cave *paintings* so far discovered are thirty-five thousand years old.   Judging by the many pre-historic paintings and carvings, there were plenty of career opportunities for artists and artisans among these hunter-gatherers. Having no paint tubes, no canvasses or frames, the Stone Age peoples kept their powdered ochre, hematite and manganese in bone cylinders and applied it moist with brush and blowpipe to hard surfaced rock walls.

Since prehistory, art has played an important role in human society, speaking to our ancestors in a vocabulary that resonated with them.   The yet to be discovered traceable starting point for art probably dissects the point with which humans emerged. From the beginning humans found methods for communicating ideas in their art which were incommunicable before its development. An artwork speaks a language of its own: it is a visual thought of an artist, and that art-thought is communicating something to each individual who sees it.

The peoples of the Stone Age are the originators of representational art, but along with realistic pictures of saber tooth tigers, bison, mammoth and horses, there are pictures of stick figure men spearing animals for food and mysterious signs and designs. Symbols that are taken for granted today were reverently invented by ancient artists. Looking at the sun and moon, for instance, the circle was possibly used to indicate unity, the cycles of the seasons, and later, the presence of a deity. It is believed that the spiral was used as a symbol of mystery and concentric rings served as stories of birth and death.

The Magical, the Mystical and Art

The role of artists as communicators of the mythic and the real was a power that can be seen in the cave paintings and small bone and stone carvings that they left behind. Nothing really explains the admirable realism of the animals painted on cave walls, the quick sure lines of the human stick figures, the layers of images superimposed on one another, or the naturalistic shapes of the earliest stone and bone carvings. But today we can still recognize the masterful artistic skills, and if we are lucky enough to see some of the Stone Age art work in person, we understand that these works mark a high achievement for humans. Their artwork stands as the remnant of a phase of enlightened development in prehistory. If great

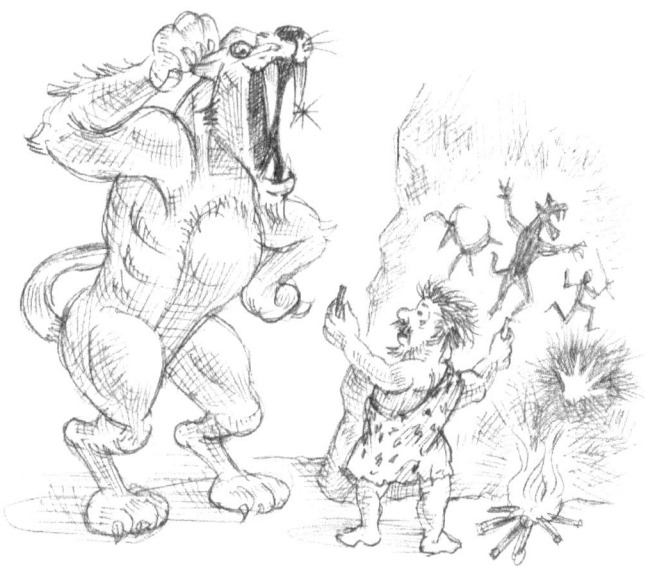

art is a timeless image which influences the way people see the world, then the unidentified works of the artists of thirty five thousand years ago can be called great.

13

Looking like the artwork of prehistoric cathedrals, the paintings were created in enormous underground chambers, far from the living places of the people who venerated them. The cave was a sanctuary where humans could contemplate the pictures and stand in awe in the face of their mystery and beauty. The images on their walls served for hunting magic, but also served as pictures for reverence and undoubtedly were connected with celebratory religious rites.

Some contemporary art historians see modern art as the "new" religion, with artists of today taking the place of priests. In this view, the artist's job is to clarify the truth and to tell the truth. But, as we can see, this is not a revolutionary post-modern idea but an idea that dates back millennia.

The Urge to Collect

Dating back not quite as far, but far enough, is the inclination for collecting artworks. Surprisingly, the human penchant for gathering, retaining and displaying collectibles is not limited to our species. Somewhere in the rainforests of New Guinea there is a bowerbird arranging a ground nest of walls of vertically placed sticks with brightly colored objects. The decorative objects he has collected include hundreds of various shells, splashily pigmented flowers, brightly patterned feathers, sparkly stones, discarded plastic items of various hues, shiny coins, used nails and pieces of colored glass. The bowerbird spends hours and hours arranging this collection which will eventually look like the equivalent of a diminutive Disneyesque amusement park hut. The bird's collection is eclectic and does not reflect a general bowerbird trend but rather is a reflection of the bird's individual taste. The bowerbird's enthusiastic propensity for displaying his idiosyncratic collection is limited only by his ability to collect the objects in the first place. For this, he often searches far and wide for just the right items and at times, steals the brightly colored bling from other bowerbird nests.

The First Collections

Let's look into the human equivalent of a Bowerbird nest: in this example the museum is an established one; the paintings on its walls range from fifteenth century dark Madonnas, through the Netherlandish art of the seventeenth century with its paintings of feasts complete with fruit and human skulls, to many centuries of pictures of nude women wearing only dignified, affected smiles and wispy material which is magically attached to appropriate body parts. There are hundreds of paintings on display and thousands more artworks in storage. The collection is famous and, within public opening hours, is accessible to all. Museums in our contemporary times are like National Parks, everyone is encouraged and even expected to appreciate the scenery. But was it always this way? How did museums become the popular edifices they are today? And what is it they really stand for anyway?

Amassing, Assembling, Accumulating

For large numbers of people, collecting "things" is a seductive and enticing pastime. There are so many tempting collectables: stamps, shoes, ties, sharks' teeth, African masks, baseball cards, taxidermic birds, masterpiece paintings, animal skeletons, family photographs, etc., etc. Collecting objects as opposed to merely *accumulating* them is one of our primal attributes and, as we shall see, can be one of our frailties.

The thing that connects the collectors of the past with the collectors of today is that they are motivated and enthused by the belief that the collected objects need to be viewed; that they are so valuable that others must take notice, that their very existence in the collection is a manifestation of their importance and value. Bizarre or beautiful, historical artifacts or artistic endeavors, the act of preserving and displaying these objects has been the chief interest of thousands if not millions of people through the ages.

Ancient peoples have kept their collecting a secret, but fanciful guessing can imagine carved and painted colorful stones lying on the floors of crude huts, preserved and maintained for the enjoyment of other tribal members.

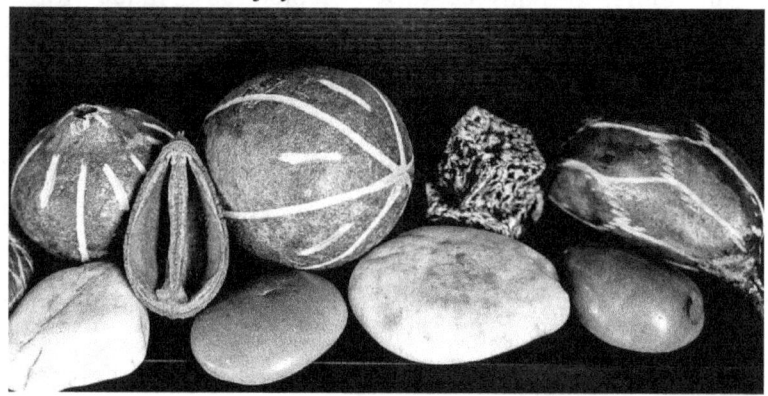

Museums: A Brief Overview

Within historical times the origins of museums are better documented. Far from being the publically accessible collections they are today, the first museum collections were the province of the privileged classes and their backroom cabinets. The great churches of Europe were where the masses of people from all walks of life were invited to attend, whereas the owners of the first historically significant collections allowed the prerogative of looking at their precious objects by invitation only. However, it was the start of museums.

Privileged Italian gentlemen of the Renaissance have been documented as developing what has eventually grown into the museum of today. Some of the collected objects were artworks, but the majority were objects with "scientific" interest. Since most people in Renaissance times did not travel extensively and science at the time was in an inchoate state, the objects collected from far and wide were "curiosities."

Many of the objects would simply be called "curious" by the twenty-first century visitor. For instance, not knowing what to make of the early discoveries of the remains of dinosaur bones, the Renaissance collector might well classify it as some ancient beastie which still roamed the outer forests where their fortified manor house was located. All manner of things were collected, categorized and stored in drawers. The first documented scientist/collector, Ulisse Aldrovandi, (1522 – 1605) had over four thousand drawers in his curiosity room with, it is assumed, far more objects than he could ever place on display.

Open to the Public...Conditionally

Publicly accessible museums appeared in Europe in the seventeenth and eighteenth centuries. These museums were actually only nominally open to the general populace. In the late 1700s, for instance, only the middle and upper classes could gain entrance to the British Museum, and to get in they had to apply in writing. An admission ticket could take up to two weeks to be mailed for the privilege of a visit that was restricted to no more than two hours.

One of the first public museums in the United States was the Revolutionary-War-era-collection of Charles Willson Peale of Philadelphia. Originally founded in his home in 1786,

Peale's collection consisted of glass showcases of illustrative hangings, three-headed snakes, a free standing North American woolly "mammoth" and many paintings of George Washington, Revolutionary War heroes, and the influential and powerful people of the era, all painted by Peale's own hand. Though the collection was moved to a public building, it was never a money-making venture. Peale eventually suffered a reversal of fortune: unable to get financial help and weighed down with the burden of artifacts, the museum failed. After his death, much of Peale's museum was sold to the showman Phineas T. Barnum.

The Greatest Show on Earth

In 1841 P.T. Barnum had purchased *Scudder's American Museum*, located on Broadway in New York City. Barnum renamed it "*Barnum's American Museum*," upgrading the building and adding exhibits. The Barnum brand of museum combined entertainment with artworks and

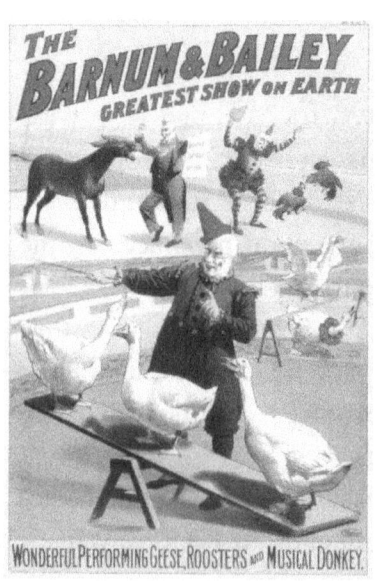

WONDERFUL PERFORMING GEESE, ROOSTERS AND MUSICAL DONKEY.

documented scientific objects. His museum became a wildly popular showplace. Barnum added outdoor "lights" by using a lighthouse lamp on the roof which shone at night; presumably one of the first buildings to give Broadway its nighttime commercial mystique. In the daytime Barnum attracted people's attention up and down Broadway with strategically placed flags along the building's roof's edge. Strolling

18

through the multistoried structure and passing by a shooting gallery and a merry-go-round, the visitor could wind up on the rooftop of the Barnum museum and pay for a twice daily ride in a hot-air balloon. There was a changing series of live acts, amusements and curiosities, including albinos, giants, midgets, jugglers, magicians, bearded ladies, detailed models of cities, models of famous battles, and exhibits of stuffed animals. By late 1846 Barnum was making so much money on his museum venture that he bought several other museums, including Peale's museum in Philadelphia.

"Curiosities" of a bizarre nature, scientific specimens, educational materials, artworks of merit, kinetic amusement rides and daily live entertainment all mingled in a show business-type-museum which proved enormously popular with the average person. New Yorkers as well as people from the rest of the nation mixed with tourists from far away countries, all flocking to the Barnum museum-as-menagerie. Each visitor was willing to pay a dime for admission to what would eventually morph into "The Greatest Show on Earth." By the mid-nineteenth century *Barnum's American Museum* was drawing four hundred thousand visitors a year.

Obviously pandering to the plebeian mindset, twenty-first century visitors might sneer at Barnum's carnie-style museum as being declassee. Yet, there remain traces of the Barnum approach in the *infotainment* of many exhibits in American museums to this day, where contemporary visitors are informed and engaged and yet within the museum's presentation, a high priority is placed on entertainment.

A More Modern Approach for Museums

More sober-minded people were also at work in the mid-nineteenth century and their inclinations and persuasions were entirely at odds with the Barnum-style museum. The cognoscenti, the well-traveled, the affluent and the civic minded... keepers of the flame for privilege or knowledge, began to think of ways other than commercial enterprise and entertainment to display collections of artworks and scientific objects.

Though the new enlightened philosophy for American museums was in the air, it was a British scientist by the name of James Smithson who set the wheels in motion. Though living in England, when Smithson wrote his will he bequeathed a large amount of money (over ten million dollars in today's currency) to the United States government for the "establishment of the increase and diffusion of knowledge among men." The Smithsonian Museum's beginnings date from 1846. Ironically, the scientist/benefactor Mr. Smithson never visited the U.S. and so never saw the rudimentary beginnings of the museum named after him.

The ideas in Smithson's museum bequest eventually became the doctrinaire ethics of the new, large public access museums: *to educate*. More, there was an undercurrent of *noblesse oblige* in this sociological outlook. No more would there be carnie-style dime museums. Instead, the museums would change and uplift the general public who were thought to be an under-educated horde in need of illumination. For this goal the large museums compiled numerous books and added libraries. The consensus was that the reason why museums should *really* exist was to form and shape the public's minds.

Helping out the General Public

With the rise of multimillionaires in the Gilded Age, the philosophy of philanthropy was coalescing into a unified whole in nineteenth century America. Andrew Carnegie, one of the wealthiest men in the history of the United States and an industrialist turned humanitarian wrote the doctrine of "The Gospel of Wealth." Carnegie was a charismatic figure and as influential in his day as Bill Gates or Steve Jobs. "The Gospel of Wealth" urged self-made people who accumulated riches from the Industrial Revolution to spend at least the last third of their life giving away their money to worthwhile causes. Carnegie wrote: "There is no class so pitiably wretched as that which possesses money and nothing else… Money can only be the useful drudge of things immeasurably higher than itself. (I) have contributed to the enlightenment and the joys of the mind…I hold this the noblest possible use of wealth."

Carnegie gave much of his fortune to the creation of free libraries but the same thought was in the minds' of the wealthy donors of the first large museums who also created edifices where admittance was free of charge. Originally closed on Sundays to assuage the more rigorous Christians on their newly established boards of directors, within a few years the museums changed their policies and opened on the Sabbath when the working class had a day off and could actually go to a museum.

The newly founded museums seemed to come just in the nick of time because, it was thought, factory workers were becoming an unruly, scrappy lot and the new institutions would be the social controllers whose collections and even very existence would tame them.

No End to the Benefit

There were exulted expectations for the newly opened museums' authority to sway public morals. Always, along with the higher principals of instruction was the underlying tone of changing public conduct: many of the early museums' founding charters contained statements pledging that they would be social guardians. The highly educated and the very wealthy were dedicated to the idea that if the workingman was allowed access to such things as scientific specimens, scientific thought, high-end artworks and classical antiquities, he would become a self-governing man whose standards would be forever elevated. Some of the anticipated behaviors which museum enthusiasts hoped to influence included everything from discouraging sex out-of-wedlock, to keeping the working family together, to stopping the family's wages being thrown away on drink.

The Giant Museums

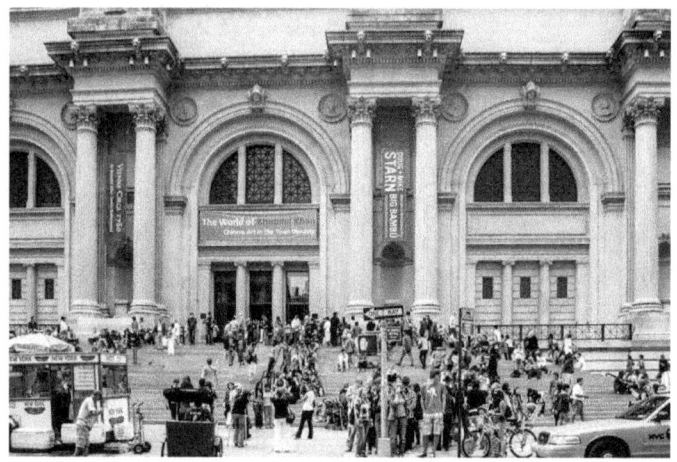

New York's Metropolitan Museum of Art

The largest of the big United States museums devoted entirely to art opened in 1872 with the founding of the Metropolitan Museum of Art in New York City. Not unlike its contemporaneous turn-of-the-century science and natural history museums, it was established by a group of wealthy businessmen and financiers who wanted to open a museum to bring art and art education to the public for the betterment of society. With the help of leading artists and thinkers of the day, the Met (as it is reverentially called), brought with it the intent to create exhibits of aesthetic worth as well as educational value. That some of the Met's exquisite collection might have been acquired through nefarious means seems to belie its initial intention of serving the public good. Outside the purview of this book, but interesting to consider, is the accusation that much of its original collection came from benefactors who, not unlike the rainforest bowerbirds, filled the Metropolitan's coffers with plundered ancient relics. (See *Rogues' Gallery* by Michael Gross for an entertaining if shocking read.)

Nevertheless, considering that at present the Metropolitan Museum of Art sustains a permanent collection of more than two million works, we can be fairly certain, given the sheer numbers, that at least to some incalculable degree the original intent of educating and uplifting the public has been, and continues to be, fulfilled.

The Purpose and How it Changed

Collections in museums exert subtle pressures on viewers; it is the fine art of persuasion. In the sixteenth to eighteenth centuries when museums were established to blend curiosities, and scientific "wonders" with artworks, the persuasive message was that fine art was no more important than the other objects and oddities. Very early artists, usually vassals to a noble, were expected to paint furniture and kitchen walls as well as originate designs and create religious altars. This is why the earliest works are not signed. Though very early collectors thought of artists as obscure and unimportant subordinates, the later collectors and the museums which began displaying artworks to elevate the masses, placed the artist's status much higher in importance.

The notions of the functions of collections and museums began to change once again in the early part of the twentieth century as the concept of the truly modern museum was born. It is no coincidence that World War 1 and the Great Depression had occurred prior to the beginnings of the modern art museums of today. Emotional truths were changing and dramatic new ideas about art were developing.

Forceful Women and the Creation of Modern Museums

Much of what was to become modern art and the changed concept of the function of museums was spurred by a cadre of women on the East Coast who changed the face of American museums. Women like Gertrude Vanderbilt Whitney (Whitney Museum of American Art), Lillie Bliss (Museum of Modern Art), Mary Quinn Sullivan (Museum of Modern Art), and Abby Rockefeller (Museum of Modern Art), contributed their significant influence, wealth, and tireless enthusiasm to promoting contemporary art and artists. These women personally *knew* the artists whose works they were collecting and endorsing. They were admirers of these modern artists long before official recognition was conferred upon them by the caretakers of the older, established museums.

Most of the modern art museums of today grew out of the intimate connections that these women collectors had with the living artists with whom they associated. The founders of the new museums were closely connected with the artworks they gifted to the new structures designed for their avant-garde works. The modern art museums were created then, out of an

24

egalitarian desire by the founders to share with the public the works they were collecting from the progressive European and American artists of the time.

Trying to Stop the Change

Just because such institutions as the Museum of Modern Art, which opened in 1929, or the Whitney, which opened in 1931, were devoted to displaying modernist artworks didn't mean that every American was on board the mother ship. For instance, in 1936 a large group of representational artists and their supporters created a national alliance called *The Society for Sanity in Art*. Its members strongly opposed all forms of modern art including cubism, surrealism, and abstract expressionism. The Society had major branches in such cities as Boston and San Francisco and their rather naive hope was that the Society's associates would influence the world enough that it would turn the tide of the collectors' enthusiasm for modern art. It didn't.

Museums of Today are Big Business

Currently, there are over seventeen thousand five hundred museums in the United States. Counting art galleries, the majority of these museums are dedicated to displaying artworks. Today, all types of art museums are not only popular, but are also big business, attracting visitor dollars and hosting millions of guests every year. Of the world's most visited art museums, the United States ranks second only to the United Kingdom in number of visitors per year: in the year 2011, over twenty eight million people visited American art museums.

In a capitalist system, fine art can be looked at in many ways; a hobby, a recreational activity, something to collect and/or a product. The museum of today has a wide ranging agenda: in its less flattering role as fund raiser, questions and criticisms sometimes arise as to the influence that contributions play in its decisions; in its more favorable role, art museums give millions of people opportunities to enjoy, participate and learn from the many interesting exhibits and activities. Visitors can come to an art museum to see the art, enjoy a concert, attend a wine tasting, see a film, watch a dance performance, attend a lecture, have a gourmet meal, eat a deli sandwich, or participate in a hands-on art program. The visitors' children can use the museum's activity rooms, work on hands-on electronic interactive games, take art classes, have a birthday party or sign up for a museum sleepover. And always, usually free of charge, the visitors can take a docent tour of the museum.

In the Next Chapters...

We have looked at the human urge to create and the human urge to collect: we have briefly explored the roots of art and the historical record of museums. In the next few chapters we will look at the urge to explain and the many and varied consequences of choosing the pursuit of becoming a tour guide in an art museum.

Chapter Two

As the docent was walking through the 17ᵗʰ century Dutch paintings, she remarked to her tour group that the women artists of that time were not allowed to paint nude. Later she felt the pang of remorse: "If only I had added the letter "s" to the last word."

Docent Standards

Docent Influence

There are entire books written by and for museum professionals…there are websites dedicated to museum education…yet, amazingly, there is very little attention given to helpful books for docents.

An art museum is not a monolith but a mosaic where many people play a part. The docent is an essential part of that mosaic. If you walk into a museum and see only its structure and staff offices, you might think that docents do not have much influence. But if you ask visitors what moved them to become a member of the museum, to donate to the museum, or to return to the museum to look at various exhibits, many times it was the docent who was the prime mover. The docent's demeanor and quality of tour is an important factor to any museum's reputation. The presence of a docent politely asking visitors to carefully look at an artwork can cause a change in the way visitors grasp the meaning of a piece of art…a work they might easily have walked past. The docent's responsibility then, is to bring an active visual experience and understanding to the group they are touring.

Who Makes a Good Docent?

Who would make a good docent? Stumbling upon one's ability to become a good docent is like waking up one day and realizing that within you there is a deep internal pool of dramatic talent: you never know the aptitude exists until there is a call. There are a myriad of personality types that might equate with a worthy docent persona: the multiplicity and variety are as vast as leaves on a tree.

The ability to empathize, to talk to others…these are traits that are essential. Flexibility is also of upmost importance since a docent might be called upon to talk to young students at one time and sophisticated adults at another. Things change swiftly with museum tours; it is the water in which a docent swims. The less flexible docents might be left behind as small tsunamis dramatically alter the situation. Next time you are at the museum, look closely at the tours and you might see some of the people in a group float past a tour guide they perceive as less than current and aware.

Which museum holds the Mona Lisa?

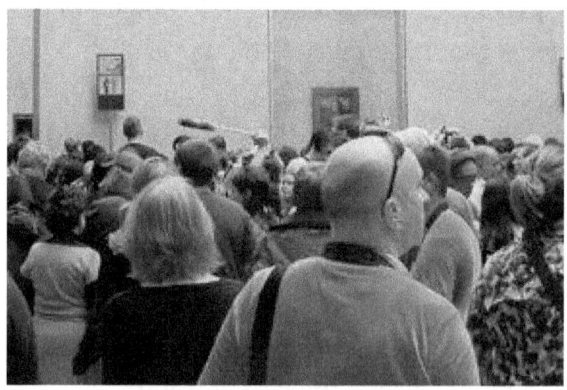

Crowds looking at the Mona Lisa

There are no knowledge-based quizzes to predict if a person will make a good docent. People who have rarefied degrees in fine art and art history make up only a small percentage of the many people who become excellent docents. Equally possible as candidates are people who have traversed different worlds of knowledge, knowledge that at first glance is seemingly far afield from the subject of art. Uniqueness comes in many flavors, and people from diverse disciplines add their own expertise, aptitude and instinct into the mix. Since a docent makes a case for each artwork, adding one's own inimitable appreciation to a presentation raises the docent bar and brings a new freshness to the museum experience.

Educators are always welcome in the docent community. Although the time has passed for museums to be limited to pedagogy as their sole purpose, education is still a crucial component for the museums of the twenty-first century. The definition of education in an art museum is now much broader and encompasses, among many other things, outreach, diversity, tours for the physically challenged, tours for people with Alzheimer's and tours for the blind and the deaf.

The Guide on the Side

Enthusiasm is an element that cannot be overlooked when thinking about important docent traits. There is no doubt that the museum visitor of any age is charmed and drawn into the creative world of art by a docent who displays a fundamentalist zeal and the ability to clarify without a cheat sheet.

There are other attributes that count highly in the docent checklist of aptitudinal characteristics. The list is similar to a description of those traits necessary when creating the public persona of a teacher or a politician; the ability to tell a story and the ability to talk with others in a friendly manner, the ability to be a good host and a good listener, the ability to rapidly read an audience and audience reactions. At times the docent is required to pull out an arcane piece of scholarship to amaze and astonish. At other times the docent will need to talk about the current topics that run through the spectrum of today's public taste. This is where knowledge of *the mojo of now* comes in handy.

In all cases, for the art works, the docent must use words. There will be approved words, there will be inappropriate words, there will be descriptive words that move the narrative along, and there will be words that bring a sense of humor to the tours. When out on the museum floor the docent won't be able to call for a lifeline. Words will be essential because they are the reason the visitor chooses a tour guide. Words are the glue that holds the tour together. Words are the human factor: much attention must be paid to them.

Where is the Visitor?

On any given day, only a small percentage of people in the U.S. are at the art museums: some of the no-shows who have planned on coming to the museum are suffering from the eternal, unending power of sloth. Many of the rest are on the road, at the malls, in their places of work, at school, at home perched in front of their electronic devices, etc.

Who is the Visitor?

The docent stands in the museum halls, waiting for an audience. Unlike the visitors of the past, many of whom were undereducated and easily awe-struck, the twenty-first century visitors to an art museum are made up of knowledgeable college groups, electronically hip school children, well-traveled tourists, east coast preppies, nerds, art aficionados, geeks, buses of senior citizens, west coast socialites, culturally concerned parents, yuppies, techno art enthusiasts, dating hopefuls; the list goes on and on.

Looking for the Deluxe Deal

Of course, there are visitors who want to wander through a museum collection on an unscripted, a la carte visit. But there are always many who would prefer a tour. The art works are the main attraction. The tours will not dissolve

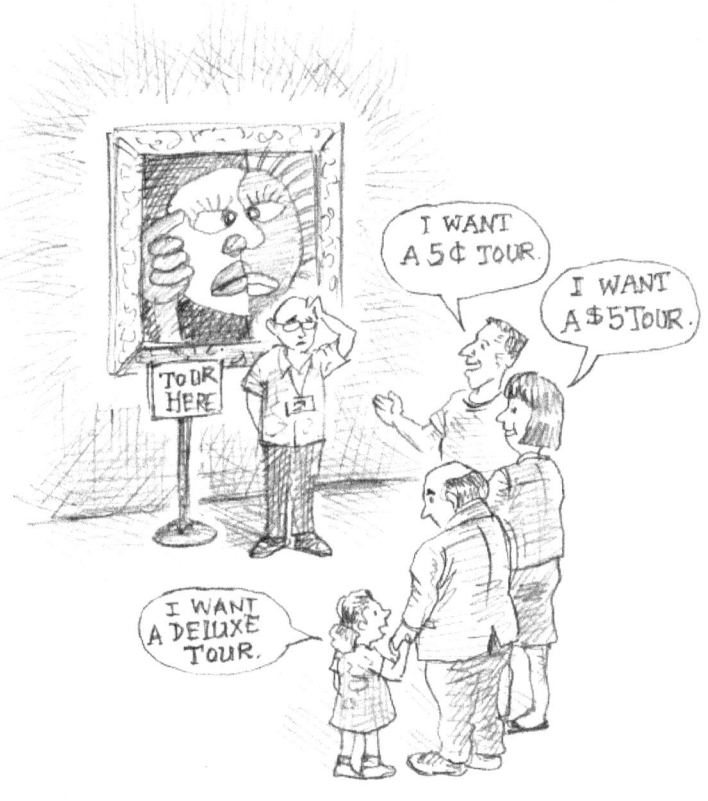

wrinkles nor remove belly fat, but they remain a draw. It is crass, but true that among the reasons docent tours are popular is because the tours are almost always free. Other than an art museum, where can a visitor find a wonderful talk, in the presence of great works of art with zero commercials? Still, visitors expect a lot of their docents. They want to know what type of tour they will be given; the fifty cent, the five dollar or the deluxe.

Docent Training

Docents generally undergo an intensive training process at the expense of the museum. The first half of the bell curve usually consists of classes in communicative and interpretive skills as well as an introduction to the institution's collection and its historical significance. The new docents are also provided with reading material that adds basic information about the art. In addition, the trainee will "shadow" an experienced docent to study how tours are given before ultimately conducting his or her own tour.

There is a docent training program in each art museum that helps manage the twists and turns of touring circumstances. Though the length of the training programs for docents varies from museum to museum, and goes from weeks to months to years, there is a common philosophy that each museum's education department will impart to the trainees.

One of the most significant lessons will be the unified curatorial position, placing the various museum pieces into the sanctioned list of artworks in the collection. Whether giving a school tour to third grade students or an adult tour to amateur artists, the curatorial position helps orient the tour to the talking points.

From Apprehension to Dread

Those who have serious problems with rejection should think long and hard before turning in their application to become a docent. On the Richter scale of terror, performance anxiety having to do with rejection might be the most difficult to overcome. Though the artworks are dwelling in a peaceful oasis of quiet and calm, waiting for the docent to bring the necessary focus for admiration or understanding, total acceptance at all times is unlikely to occur. A positive reception is the general rule, but when giving a tour there may sometimes be a museum visitor who is both a skeptic and is vocal about it. Inside the docent's outer clothing, a thick, all-weather skin is the best shield. The docents who are polite yet firm and secure in their tour information will not be cowed. And one unconvinced visitor might actually be beneficial to the docent, giving the docent a chance to practice tolerance and listening. There are different ways to see: understanding other's points of view makes us reflect on our own set of truths. Remembering that no one has the inalienable, indestructible doctrinaire version of truth will help the docent give straightforward, honest responses.

Student Educational Methods: A Mix with Different Colors

The docent trainee is given information, methods and techniques for dealing with school group tours. Generally, art museums set up educational programs that emphasize social learning. Much of the information is focused on the ability of the docent to encourage the use of inquiry, dialogue and play. Many of the educational programs will be changeable as the winds, as new methods blow in and then recede only to be replaced by a flurry of newer methods.

One of the more tried-and-true techniques is a version of Visual Thinking Strategies (VTS) which stresses a content free tour. Much like the Socratic Method, this is a questioning procedure that attempts to cultivate a culture of thinking by using a set of well-crafted questions. Student visitors who are given this teaching method automatically begin to think in terms of providing evidence. Though there is no tour that is entirely content free, VTS focuses on the student's own interpretation of an artwork without additional information from the docent.

Unfortunately, like the original Socratic Method which added so little content that Socrates was accused of being a sophist, the docent can overdo the use of VTS. One child, having gone through an entire tour where the docent used only the questioning method, finally became so frustrated that she asked, "Do you know anything at all about art, or are you just an asker?" Luckily for the docent, the student did not have a vial of hemlock with her.

Touring in the Techno Age

In the fertile field of education, up-to-date training for new as well as experienced docents is fluid. Now, more than ever, the world of technology is part of the everyday life of the museums' education departments, and "digital" is the biggest news in the field. Terms like "free-choice learning" have to do with the many ways in which the virtual world has stimulated autonomous ideas. In this new age of technology it will be the docent who is trained to link the student's familiar virtual world to the concrete world of collections and exhibitions.

In some important ways, education is the most revolutionary aspect of museums, encompassing exploration, study, observation, critical thinking, contemplation and dialogue. There are many inventive teaching solutions that are continually being created to help students participate in and be inspired by the world of art. Museum education is constantly morphing: the transformation as to what is current and deemed necessary might change in the blink of an eye. This is the new reality, waters of change run swiftly through modern-day touring. With the help of the museum's education department, the more adaptable docents will be able to navigate the choppy waters and master the new methods needed to keep afloat.

The Adult Visitor and Docent Difficulties

Leave your backpack, purses and large bags at the desk is a sign often seen in art museums. It is easier to leave an item of clothing in the cloakroom than it is to leave one's personality at the front door. The museum visitor's mind never comes in tabula rasa form. Instead, people view art on their own terms. Like an expensive car, the adult museum visitor comes fully equipped. This very fact sometimes makes docent work challenging. Visitors outfitted with their own opinions, assumptions and suppositions may pose a variety of difficulties for a docent.

Some problems that a docent might encounter are:

People unaccustomed to museums Not having visited art museums, it is easy to view paintings as wall decorations. You might hear a visitor say, "I don't like that painting because it wouldn't fit in with the colors in my living room." The challenge for the docent will be to bring a bigger view into focus.

An overload of culture When visitors traverse the galleries of an art museum for the first time, the many artworks themselves make the visual world a confusing conglomeration. The challenge is to see that the visitor is not being overwhelmed.

One person in the group has been dragooned into going to the museum The attitude of the person who was coerced into attending the exhibition is more funereal than attentive. For the multi-talented docent, perhaps humming a few bars of a song and a small tap dance might revive this type of visitor.

Children's Tours

Children's tours can be a refreshing change, but the breeze that blows may turn into a whirlwind. Young students have intense but short attention spans. And since most students are not familiar with museum rules and are filled with uninhibited excitement, the challenge is to give them food for thought while enforcing standards of behavior.

Behavioral standards that seem obvious to a sophisticated adult might not seem reasonable to a child. When students get off a school bus to visit a museum, they think of themselves as being on a vacation from school rules, also known as a "field trip." It is possible that the docent in charge of their group will be seen as the tyrannical official who must read them the equivalent of the museum's Miranda rights: "You have the right to remain silent unless you raise your hand." "You have the right to confine yourself to your group and have an enjoyable museum experience." The prophylactic notification sounds like information any victim is required to receive once in protective custody: no touching or defacing museum property; no use of cell phones or other electronic devices; no eating and drinking except in designated areas; no loud or disruptive noises; no offensive language or gestures. **Can't a kid have any fun?**

The role of docent-as-enforcement-officer interferes with the docent's role as educator and guide. It can be a juggling act and one that a docent will need to be prepared for if the school group has not been given the standards of behavior beforehand by their overworked and harried teachers.

The Stewardship of the Artwork

Responsible maintenance, care and preservation of the art works is the task and obligation of the museum. When on duty as a docent, the job of safekeeping the museum's works becomes one of the functions of the docent as well. It is a job that most docents take on willingly: the museum's objects are carefully placed with thoughtful museum labels, in specific positions in the galleries. They are cleaned, dusted, polished and if necessary tinkered with, adjusted and riveted in place by museum staff. By their very presence in the museum's collection the artworks are deemed important. Though it is necessary to always keep this in mind, enjoyable viewing experiences for the public must also be considered. Museum guards are helpful when something egregious looks as if it is about to happen.

Though constant vigil of the collection is a good rule to follow, there is a limit for any docent as to how much emergency preparedness and response one is obligated to do. Balancing the docent standards with what is sensible touring practice in individual situations will always require multi-tasking. The objective for the docent is to keep the surveillance subtle and not look like a member of homeland security.

The Docent Experience; Unmatched Satisfaction

Though docents with many years under their belts will have encountered a myriad of circumstances, most will tell you that there are very few pursuits which expand the mind and warm the heart as much as docent work in an art museum. The museum studies invariably include vast amounts of information about fine art, art history, and related fields. Liberated and released from the strictures of academia, the docent is free to digest and interpret the scholastic information in their own way. Continual learning is not only inevitable, but enjoyable. Free from tests and formalized boundaries, the docent becomes a generalist in mind and expertise. This rich experience has the potential for unparalleled intellectual transformation.

Another benefit of docent work is that under most circumstances there is no need for a lockstep mindset when you give your museum tours. Within certain parameters, docents usually are free to choose the works in the museum according to their own knowledge and preferences. In a sense, docents invent their tours. This allows them to decide whether they like the forest, or prefer the trees.

As unwieldy as the interaction with others can occasionally be, there is nothing to compare with the docent and group who have the right chemistry. The dynamic relationships that are built, brief though they are, cannot help but inspire. As a docent, you can bask in the knowledge that you have made a serious contribution to other's abilities to look at the art in the museum with eyes that see deeply and hearts that you have helped to open.

Docent work is always a collaborative effort. It is an oxygen rich environment; working within the community of the many other docents and in a joint effort with the education department will bring rewards of its own, as well as gain many exciting new friends.

In the Next Chapter...

In this chapter we have seen that docent standards are pliable, elastic and encompassing. The standards are there as guideposts, but are accepting of many people from a variety of walks of life. Though there are occasional challenges posed by the viewing public, the docent is frequently enlivened by these experiences. The standards cannot solve each isolated problem but the learning curve, once climbed, is itself protective and helpful.

In the next chapter we will talk about how much a beginning docent needs to know about art and art history and how much the essential nature of an artistic mind plays in basic comprehension of the works. Also discussed will be the practical reality of the affordability of becoming a docent.

Chapter Three

We must declare ourselves, become known; allow the world to discover this life…which connects farm boys, artists and clerks. Let them see that the important thing is not the object of love but the emotion itself.
Gore Vidal

What Is Necessary to Know?

Sorting Out Docent Qualifications

Ask yourself these questions:

- Have you found art museum experiences to be memorable?
- Has going to an art museum inspired you?
- Have you shared your interest in art with other people?
- Have you ever hoped to influence and arouse others by telling them about a favorite work of art that you saw?

Chances are you have positive responses to some of these questions. If you think of what your answers imply, it will be obvious that you are a qualified candidate to apply to become a docent in an art museum.

The Docent and Knowledge of Art

A doubt about whether art docent activity is desirable sometimes takes this form: is it necessary that a docent be knowledgeable in art history? Does one have to be someone who can identify art works at forty paces? At first glance this prerequisite might seem as if it were advantageous. It may be, but how realistic is this assumption?

One obvious problem is that finding the person with "perfect" qualifications for docent work is as likely as finding the fundamental forces and elementary particles missing in Einstein's Unified Field Theory. There are many ways into which art can be parsed, from early art all the way through to contemporary visions. For the most part, these diverse approaches are shaped by critics and historians. One could spend a lifetime studying the ways in which artists have composed their works, or historians have identified works of art, or analyzing how broad art movements fit into cultural clusters.

At times the experts themselves differ as to classifications. For instance, classifications become a thorny issue when there is disagreement about the work of an artist whose accomplishments do not fit into prescribed categories. Shifting details and particulars make studying art and its history both exhilarating and complex. To find a docent candidate with a limitless grasp of all the subtleties of art history is impossible because such a person does not exist.

The Dedicated Experts

Of course, there are trained specialists in art and art history. They are commonly found in the halls of academe or on the staff of an art museum. They frequently have several letters after their surnames; appellations which are useful in accrediting and designating them to other scholars. These specialists sort, categorize, rate and write. They are able to explain how a work was painted, how a painting was restored, what happened around the time and in the place where the work was created, its provenance, of what the artist's compendium consists, etc. The art specialists do an admirable job of getting to the academic heart of the matter.

Aesthetics versus Art History

Yet some serious problems in clarity can exist in the explanations given by the academics. Statements implicitly grasped by scholars may not be entirely understandable to the general museum visitor. It is, on some basic level, a public relations problem. Visitors to an art museum come with varying degrees of knowledge, sensibilities and interests in art. This is where the job of a docent is the strongest, since it is a docent's job to bring a level of understanding commensurate with the visitors' own reference points. There is no possibility that a docent could get visitors to see through the eyes of an expert. Trying to explain in specialist's terms would only confuse and obfuscate. It is a docent's duty to make sure that if anyone's head spins around it is theirs and not that of the visitors.

There is also a possibility in which a specialist's knowledge of history breeds a standardized acceptance and approval of works of art without the beginner's appreciation and innocent emotional response.

Not needing to form the same bonds with scholarship, the visitor might not know the accepted notions of what is fitting or desirable. Not bound by the same strictures as the scholars, without knowing pre-set academic principles, without much knowledge of the rules, it is possible to fall in love with a work of art in a non-sensible, passionate sort of way; a way that is only possible with an unadorned mind. This type of enthusiasm can be used by a docent: as a non-specialist and lover of art, the docent has the capacity to persuade with a fervor that might elude a more reserved academic.

Art: The Fabric of Life

Art is part of the fabric of living, we encounter it everywhere. Art is being created all around us, daily opening our eyes to new experiences and forcing us to adjust to new ways of viewing. Broadly speaking, art is anything consciously and imaginatively created by humans that changes one's sense of what the world is.

Below is an interview with Sara. Her words illustrate the way in which art and art museums can change one's perspective:

As an older person and art lover, I have found the changing world of art in my local museum a way to change my mind. Almost since the beginning of the cyberspace revolution it was obvious that electronics would touch many aspects of the fine arts. At first I struggled with that concept; particularly when I saw art pieces which were made with new materials and technologies. Looking at a swirling, ever-changing exhibit of dots projected on the wall of my favorite museum, I wondered just what it had to do with the art of da Vinci, Rembrandt or Turner.

I had to look very closely to see the "art" in a contemporary piece which incorporated plastic, neon lights and a blinking computer image. It was shocking. It was new. It made me uncomfortable. All the pieces and bits were so modern and extreme that when I was in their presence they almost made me dizzy.

But because I value museums and respect the people who make the selections, I have been able to overcome my initial aversion to many creations of contemporary art.

And my story doesn't stop here. Because I have opened my mind a crack, a little part of me started looking at other things differently. I noticed that some of the people whom I did not hold in the highest esteem because of their differences, didn't look as unattractive as I first thought. I haven't put on a torn tee shirt, given myself permission to have body piercings, or moved to a shabby but "hip" neighborhood, but I feel more relaxed about the people who have.
Sara P.
Iowa City, IA

Likes, Dislikes and Familiarity

Ubiquitous as art is, there is nevertheless no unified position as to how visitors will experience the works in an art museum. People accept what they are familiar with and if a certain kind of art is the only art that they know, it will be the way in which their ideas about art are molded. For instance, the commercial arts are more deeply enmeshed in most people's everyday lives. Because commercial art in the form of advertising caters to a wider audience, fine art that reflects this type of influence is very popular.

There are people who wish to stay more limited in their experience, scope and breadth: some will close their minds to all but representational art; there are young students who might only have encountered the graffiti art sprayed on buildings or the illustrations in comic books and video games; there are people who only accept art if it is the kind they have encountered when they enter their church. Nevertheless, in some form or other, art has most likely touched everyone at one time, and this is where the docent can meet the visitor.

The Fine Art of a Fine Docent

There is no doubt that for a docent there are benefits to having artistic talent. An artist is a person with an unanalyzable creative power: what separates a work of art from a blank piece of paper is the hand of the artist who created it. The creative process is a mysterious and unpredictable human activity. The artist starts with imagination; the creation which takes shape is an attempt to give that imagination form. Each time the artist adds to his creation, a new leap has been made. Gradually a visible form is defined; it is a special gift.

There are distinctive rewards for docents who are also artists. Though delineating a step-by-step account of the way a work of art was created would not be entertaining or even possible, a docent with an artistic background might very well be able to reveal some interesting aspects of an art work.

Can there be true appreciation and understanding of art without being an artist oneself? Think of the sensitive awareness and recognition of an art collector. Think of the deep comprehension of a person trained in art history or museum education. The same profound admiration of aesthetic values can be true for a docent. Though a wonderful gift, being an artist is not a prerequisite for docent work in an art museum.

Hands On: An Artistic Endeavor

The desire to achieve something original is an inclination felt by all of us sometime in our life: to that extent we all have a potential to express ourselves artistically. To the

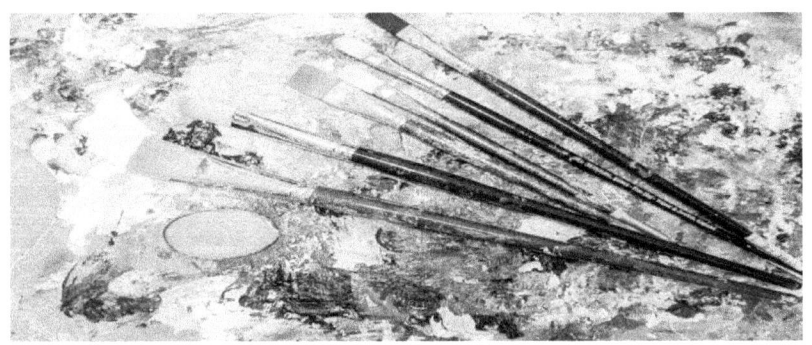

non-artist, the making of a work of art might seem a strange and dicey business: how does one choose the right line, the right color, the right form or the right perspective? Is it necessary to start out drawing naturalistic objects and figures? Assuming that not everyone will buy an easel and hire a model, or have the necessary will power and patience to attempt to draw a vase of delicate flowers, there are still ways in which, as a non-artist, you can see how it feels to inhabit the artist's world.

When a person says "I don't know anything about how to paint or draw," this thought is confirming one's own negative belief and can become a self-fulfilling prophecy. We all must know something about creating art: the fact is that nearly everyone already draws. Who has not sketched a rough map to give directions or made doodles on a Post-It note? Perhaps you "can't draw a straight line;" but you know how to write in cursive, joining successive characters with flowing strokes of a pen. There are ways in which everyone knows how to draw.

Of all the pursuits open to us, drawing is perhaps the easiest to take up, requiring only minimal equipment: a pencil and some blank paper. You might want to work on your drawing ability by attempting the following task. To get a firmer grip on the dimly felt artistic impulse, try this simple exercise:

The Signature Exercise

If you think you can't draw and will never be able to, try the following: assuming you have some sort of way to sign your name and you are not signing with an "X," you will have some sort of signature ranging from a large flourish to a small scratch. In this exercise you will only have to "draw" your signature. Take a sheet of plain typing paper and start signing your signature at the top left-hand corner. Sign a line of signatures all the way across the page. Now turn the page upside down and sign a line across the bottom of the page. Do the same thing with the other two sides, turning the paper appropriately to be able to sign your name. After you have "framed" your work you can get busy signing your name as you want, filling in the blank inner part of the page. You should feel looser now and you might feel bold enough to sign your name in many sizes and styles, using your imagination and your new-found freedom to draw. When you get done, look to see if you need to connect some of the letters or add touches such as geometrical patterns or little faces."Kilroy was here" still works; graffiti will do wonders to perk up a signature or two. When you have finished, stand back and look at your masterpiece. You have just created a drawing!

Remember that drawing is a form of art and art does not necessarily fit into neat pigeonholes. Your first steps can be merely a stage on a journey that has no end. Like life, what you get out of drawing is dependent upon what you put in.

The Possibility of Taking an Art Class

Artists sometimes teach classes not necessarily to make the students become artists, but to make them become better judges of art. After several months of wielding a paintbrush, however ineptly, one cannot help but see line and color with more depth and feeling. On these grounds, just taking an art class might help you to relate to art masterpieces differently: more than having the expectation that the student will create an "acceptable" art work, the student might find a new awareness.

Good Student/Good Docent

When visitors came to his house, the great French Fauve artist Claude Matisse used to ask, "What have you done for color today?" The question is a good one and to it could be added, "What have you done for art today?" To their credit, art docents are secure in their answer.

Can you afford to become a docent?

"I'd asked around 10 or 15 people for suggestions. Finally one lady friend asked the right question:
'Well, what do you love most?'
That's how I started painting money. "
          Andy Warhol

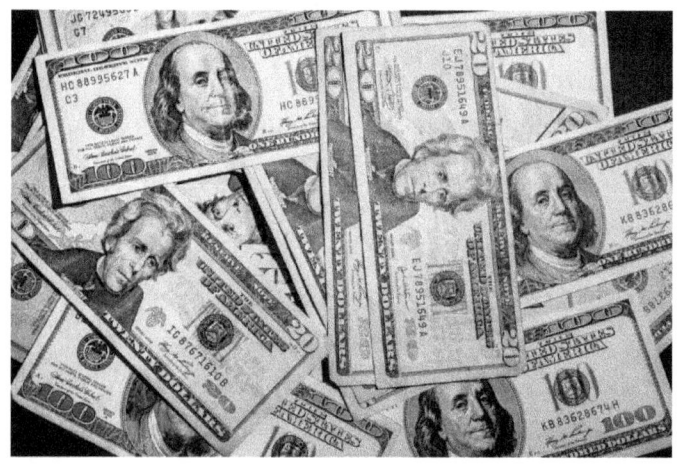

    Money....It is an interesting topic and one that is not always given much thought when considering the possibility of becoming a volunteer docent at an art museum. It is an easy subject to gloss over. Like education, one never knows exactly how much one needs for the position.

    There are always more socially acceptable reasons than cash to talk about: you want to help people discover art works in the local art museum; you hope to learn more about art and art history as you go through the mandatory training; you are interested in meeting others who share your values... it seems as easy as that.

But these are motivating factors and important as they are, the reality of available assets might be an altogether different and conflicting problem.

Here are questions that you might ask yourself before ever applying to become an art docent:

- How much will travel cost me?
- What will parking cost me?
- Will I need to buy food at a café or restaurant?
- How many new clothes will I need (if any)?
- How will I fit my job/part time job into the mix?
- How many times a month will I need to hire someone to look after my child/dog/cat/elderly parent?

A clear estimation of one's money source should play a role in any consideration of volunteer work. The cold, hard truth is that some people who wish to become docents can easily afford to follow their passions. Other would-be-docents will find that they will be juggling their personal budget by making choices about whether to buy organic vegetables or just go with the can of Campbell's chicken noodle soup that night.

The Dream of Possible Employment

It is not realistic to envision docent life as a possible springboard to a career in museum art education. Though this may happen to a very lucky few individuals, it is best not to paint yourself into this bright vision of the future. Most museums are underfunded and always, the competition to get jobs in museum work is daunting. The possibility of being disappointed is too great to risk unbridled, naive optimism.

The job of an art museum tour guide might be best clarified if looked upon as extracurricular employment. In other words, work without pay. This will give a clear idea of what is required: there will be work in the form of learning and touring and there will be responsibilities in the form of keeping up the standards of the museum.

Moving Up a Notch

It is also possible to think of docent work as a credentialing procedure; a way to climb the social ladder. Again, though such aspirations are possible, there is no way to control for the mysterious ups and downs of status. The field of docent work is rewarding, though the social payback or monetary rewards might very well be non-existent.

Being a docent also requires a good deal of hard work. When looked upon this way, there will be no mistaken views about signing up for a volunteer job which might carry with it a certain cachet, and might (incorrectly) be thought of as requiring minimal effort.

The Contribution is the Reward

The easiest way to keep a clear head about docent work is to remember that a docent volunteers in order to do the best possible job for the museum and the museum visitor. If this thought is kept in the forefront of one's mind, the return on one's sweat equity will be greatly rewarded.

Time as a Factor

You must be prepared to give up a good deal of personal time while you are attending the training classes. When the courses are completed, you will need to find time to give tours. And one's education as a docent does not stop with the initial training period. Learning about the art works and the constantly changing exhibitions is an on-going process; all of which takes up time. And time, as the saying goes, is money.

The Affordability Factor

Can you afford to become a docent? Some of the questions to ask are about daily commitments, work schedules, travel expenses and clothing expenses. Daily commitments might be anything from walking the dog, to looking after children, to caring for an elderly parent, to other volunteer activities. If employed, you should be aware of how much time you can tweak out of your schedule to allow for spaces wholly reserved for museum business.

Traveling expenses would not seem a big consideration, but the number of times it is necessary to travel to the museum, both for training and to give tours, might come as a surprise. Unless you are lucky enough to live within a few miles, you can count on traveling to and from the museum much more often than you have estimated. You have heard of cost overruns; once you are a fully functioning docent you will probably have travel overruns.

Finally, though clothing expenses do not play the same monetary role as daily commitments, work schedules and travel expenses, two things are necessary as a docent representing the museum; comfortable clothing which is also appropriate attire. There is no need to be addicted to fashion: there are always clothes at reasonable prices that will fit the role of a volunteer docent.

Pretty Bling/Not to Bring

A cautionary suggestion: the word in the docent community is that too much jewelry, pinned, fastened or clasped, and whether costume or real, is not appropriate for the touring docent to wear. For instance, wearing an exquisite and large sparkly pendant or necklace makes a powerful statement. It is possible that the flashy and precious stones will distract from the museum's art works and cause a contest in the minds of the visitors as to where to place their attention.

The Fabric of Art or Just the Fabric?
A Story

Her clothing was expensive and impeccable. Bought at the finest boutique stores, her attire reflected her life; one of comfort, ease and money.

She had been to the museum many times. Or at least she thought she had. Was it four times that she had attended an open house at the museum with friends? How charming the company. She might not remember how many times she had attended museum parties, but she distinctly remembered that fascinating young artist who flirted with her at an exhibit opening. She tried to think if she had ever really been to the museum after that. The young artist never called back. She succinctly remembered that. She was planning to go to a museum exhibit opening last year but her husband had decided they were going to spend the time in their winter home in Aspen. Oh, but surely she had been to the museum more than once. It is the type of activity one does, when one is in elevated economic circumstances.

Her husband was all for the idea when she told him: she would become an art docent. If the truth were told, her husband was for anything that kept her occupied and out of his hair. She took it as a positive sign that he approved of her new idea. After all, she loved Grandma Moses paintings. And her husband had several one-of-a-kind copies of Remington sculptures.

Yes, she would apply to be a docent. She could call Mildred, who, as President of the Museum Art Board, would put in a good word for her.

It gave her such a rush to envision her entrance into the museum. What to wear? What to wear?

"But my dear, why don't you just donate a substantial sum and get onto the Museum Board?" Mildred was saying. "If you get on the board, we can have lunch together more frequently."

"No, no," she said. She wanted to train in the ways of art. "Art has always been my passion," she said emphatically.

"Really?" asked Mildred in a bemused, indulgent fashion.

The day of the interview was exciting for her. She had picked out a very special purple suit to wear. It was one that she had bought in Paris last year and had been saving for a really special occasion. She rose early and took special care applying her cosmetics and fluffing out her coiffed hair. While attempting to fasten the purple suit coat she noticed it tugged at the button holes. Try as she would, neither the coat nor the skirt fit. Perhaps she had been too quick in buying it at that haute couture store last year and didn't notice the flaws in its manufacturing. She finally decided on wearing a common Armani outfit. By the time she put herself together, she was over an hour late for the museum interview.

Expecting to make an even grander impression as a late arrival, she entered the staff offices only to find they were interviewing other applicants. She must wait in the reception area.

As she sat in the museum, she couldn't help but look around at the artworks on the walls. This was the first time she had actually taken a look-see and she wasn't too pleased with what assaulted her eyes. There were strange modernist structures and canvasses painted with abstract drips and splashes. Farther down the building's walls she saw Old Dutch Master Paintings with flowers, moths and worms. What did all these works mean? She squirmed in her chair.

As these thoughts occurred to her, other thoughts replaced them. Wouldn't it be lovely to go out and buy a new purple suit to replace the one which inexplicably shrunk? It was so much easier to continue her present life of shopping and entertainment. Her day of art enthusiasm had passed. It was only the *thought* of becoming a docent that excited her.

What Makes the World Go Round

Happily for those of us in less than optimal monetary circumstances, becoming a docent is not a pursuit where money trumps all. Still, your financial circumstances should be a consideration.

A realistic idea of the necessary prerequisites will ensure that there will be no mistaken views about the reason for signing up for docent training. You will have a clear vision of what is needed and you will avoid the unpleasant experience of discovering that the life of a docent is not what it was cracked up to be.

You will be able to spend many years in this rewarding field and ultimately hit your full stride. At the end of your docent career you will be able to look back with the satisfaction of knowing how many adults and children you have enlightened, entertained, educated, inspired and helped adjust to the world of art. You can rest in the satisfaction of knowing that you have made an important contribution to society.

Is it worth the effort? You bet!
Can you afford it? Keep it real!

In the Next Chapter...

In this chapter we have seen that there are many life paths that lead to the pursuit of training as an art docent. There is a sliding scale of qualifications because people have various aptitudinal strengths, interests and talents that will be supportive in their endeavor to become art docents. Though far from the aesthetic life, the reality of expenses should be a consideration in volunteering, just as income and expenses are factored into the functioning and management of an art museum.

In the next chapter we will go into a discussion of the complexities, humorous incidents, challenges and joys of the docent tour itself.

Chapter Four

Tour: *A journey for pleasure or education, often involving a series of stops and ending at the starting point.* *Merriam-Webster Dictionary*

The Tour and Speaking to the Public

The museum is an old one: the paintings on its hallowed walls range from early Madonnas with large headed infants to very bleak pictures of Victorian men wearing black top hats, suits and beards. There are hundreds of paintings and they are spread out over many galleries. They are all remarkable, though the degree to which they are unique and provide historical interest varies with the opinions of the many inconstant art critics. Suffice it to say, the collection is a rare one and a Warren Buffett fortune would be needed to replace it.

Into this sanctuary of high cultural value and material possessions toddles an elderly man wielding a cane, slavishly followed by several women who are as ancient as he. The elderly man with a cane starts to circumnavigate the galleries with the women shuffling behind him. Docent Sue, alert and on duty in these galleries, notices that the elderly man is expostulating on the artworks to his lady friends. (Or perhaps the ladies are relatives? Surely, Docent Sue is thinking, one would hardly expect at this man's advanced age, that he is taking his harem out for an informational visit to the art museum.)

When the old man comes upon a painting he likes, he raises his voice in enthusiasm and abruptly lifts his cane and taps the painting. Tap. Tap.

Rushing up to him Docent Sue calls out in a raspy, nervous voice: "Sir! We do not allow the artworks to be touched."

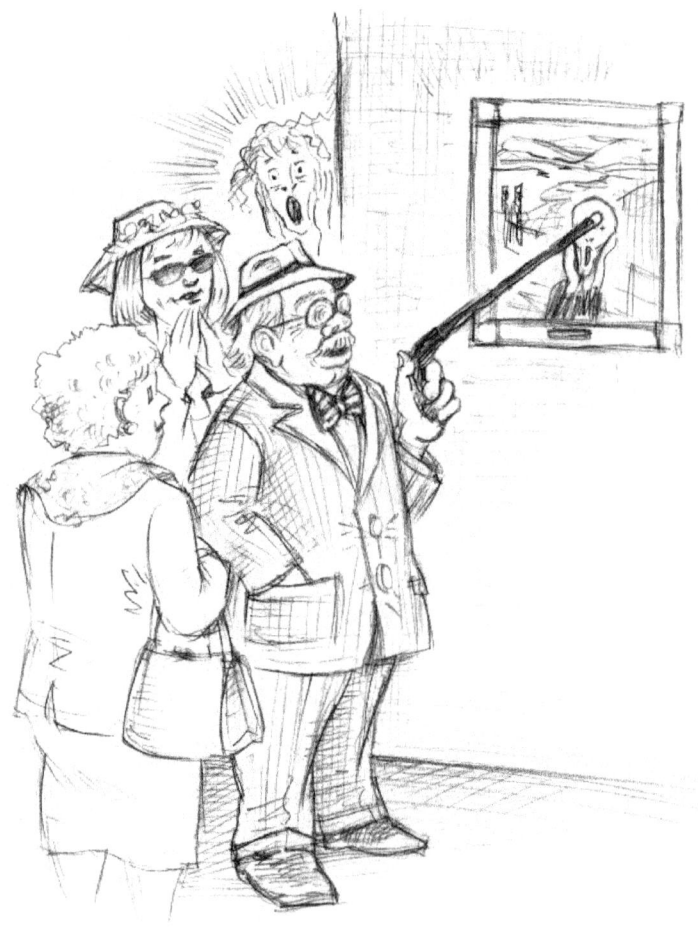

"Um, hum," the old man says, nodding his head compliantly, his feet moving perfunctorily down the corridor. His lady friends, who appear to pay no attention to Docent Sue, leisurely follow behind him. Their faces are filmed over with transparent skin that clings like dried Vaseline so that as they stand in front of a painting, they look a little like fish peering out from their bowl.

Docent Sue squints disapprovingly at this odd assemblage of women who are listening so closely to this old man that their turned-up noses tweak and tremble with every scintillating utterance. Docent Sue is forming an opinion in her mind which she would not like to share with others; an opinion that these elderly women actually *are* his unconventional "friends" and perhaps even art heretics. The air starts to ionize around Docent Sue as she eyes this band of senescent nonconformists. A gloom is settling over her.

Stopping in front of another painting and lifting his cane from the floor, again the old man slowly swings it in an arch, as if ready to begin a duel with the artwork in question. Tapping the new painting a bit harder than the last, he rapidly expostulates about its power to draw the viewer into the picture, the contrasting colors, and the artist's use of costumes in this genre scene.

With a Girl Scout's sensibilities, Docent Sue runs up to meet the eyes of this unorthodox group. Docent Sue wags her right index finger at the elderly man's face and squeezes her lips together as she vigorously shakes her head in disapproval. The gloom that settled on her a few minutes ago has turned into a sinking feeling in the pit of her torso. She is thinking that her effete efforts are useless: worse, she may have just witnessed a vandalism which she should have been able to prevent. She backs off; some things are beyond the pale of a tour guide. The memorization of the gallery notes, the hours of studying, the months of trainee preparation, all have gone for naught under the tap, tapping of one little old man's cane.

None but Docent Sue notices the two security guards rushing up to the septuagenarian group. The elderly man is being escorted to the security guard offices. The women look astonished.

"Why? Why?" they plead, now all up-turned noses moving in the direction of Docent Sue.

But Docent Sue does not want to listen. She must follow the rules. Why are these women shuffling in her direction with their arms outstretched? What can she do? She is a docent, not a big, burly guard hired by security services.

Try as she will, she cannot retreat in time. The women explain to Docent Sue that it is Professor Homes who has just been removed from the premises. He is the leading authority in some arcane art history subject. Docent Sue does not know the subject; she does not know these women who reminded her only a few minutes ago of archaic creatures out of the nether world of a Hieronymus Bosch painting.

She flees from them...down the hall and up the back stairs to the docent offices where she sits, deflated, as feelings of guilt flood over her. If only she had simply asked the Professor (what's-his-name?), if she could store his cane in the coat closet. If only she had been more determined, more certain, exhibited more strength.

Welcome to the world of the art docent tour

There are days when the tour guide is standing on the sixth rung of the ladder and days of precipitous drops. Giving docent tours is never boring and at times is not without another fine art: theatrics. It can be a world where occasional dramas are played out in front of fabulous artifacts in very public places. On occasion, a tour starts out as tragedy and mutates into mere comedy. Paraphrasing Jackson Pollock, the docent must be prepared to, "Work tight and talk loose."

The people who become docents have been diligently screened and interviewed before they are invited to participate in a training program. Only the brave need apply. It is a very public position and one that when actually engaged in, is protected only by street clothes and a good pair of walking shoes. The armor is skimpy, the danger is real.

What lies behind us and what lies before us are tiny matters compared to what lies within us.   Ralph Waldo Emerson

If Shakespeare had been a docent in Renaissance England, giving dramatic tours in some moldy medieval estate located upon a drafty hillock, he might well have said, "The *tour* is the thing."   It looms over the docent as clouds inevitably cling to high mountain tops. Though docents can wander the museum hallways answering the occasional obscure question posed by a visitor, it is the docent tour for which they have trained.   Preparation is everything to a docent.   The need for it is pressing. It is the motivation of preparation, rather than the tours themselves that many times give the inspiration.

When one is up against the exigencies of learning about a new exhibition and time is of the essence, the docent must work to the edge. For an experienced docent, the end product of a well-thought-out and well-rehearsed tour is the comfortable part of the journey.   It is what the docent has studied for. There is the heartwarming feeling one gets when the tour is over and everyone seems pleased. Light clapping can be heard through the museum corridors. That is the edge a docent is most happy walking.

Finding the Right Elements for the Mix

When explaining what it is like to be an art docent, there are analogies to draw from: a docent needs to visualize the skills of an artist; a docent needs to construct tours with the skill of a carpenter; a docent needs to make the tour sing like a musician; a docent needs to hit the mark like an archer. And if the whole tour really cooks, the docent has constructed a masterpiece like the finest chef, and the visitors have digested the tour… an achievement fit for the honored guests they are.

Finding the right ingredients is the trick to a well-run, informative docent tour. Reading the needs of the visitors—to be gladdened, to be given information and to be inspired—is like a master chef's ability to please the tastes of the people in the royal palace. Being a docent is a skill, and mastering it should be enjoyable in the same way it is to master any other rewarding pursuit.

Rewards abound for the art museum docent. Fortunately, for any visitor who is not entirely charmed with the tour, there are many more that will come away with the recompense of a significant experience. Most museum visitors go off smiling, refreshed. They have a new point of reference with which to look at the world. The docent has become a vehicle for the art.

"Everyone is lovely until you get to know them."

It must be admitted that within any group of visitors, reactions vary greatly. The visitors on a docent-led tour can be critical, fickle, receptive or enthusiastic. The group is never committed and is, of course, free to accept or reject a tour or the art. No tour guide knows in advance how an artwork will be received.

There are times when only the weary, overscheduled visitors take the tour. Their ability to be open to any discussion of art is hindered by their frazzled state of mind.

There are some visitors who will value the paintings solely on historical grounds.

Other frequent-return visitors will have nostalgic attachments to several artworks and will expect any tour to include their treasured favorites.

Among the various types of visitors, there are lovers of art and culture who choose to go on a guided tour, but ironically allow little time. Time is of the essence with these busy people. It is easy to imagine that they behave on the tour much as they would in a restaurant geared for hearty eaters; voraciously seeing as many works of art in the shortest period of time possible.

Signage Language

Even after deciding on a tour, there might be a member of the group who spends more time reading wall labels than paying attention to what is said. There is a certain logic in this way of thinking. The signage is a slippery item: it answers significant questions for the visitors. Wall labels can be reference points to navigate from one work to another. They are wayfinding signs posted with great thought by the curator, the exhibition specialist and the art historian. Because of this, the small label holds a great deal of prestige. The label might "explain" the art in a manner that can sway the visitor into a new interpretation. Some visitors are so affected by this type of authority and so practiced at reading wall labels, that they exhibit the skill of identification on the level of a logistic analytics consultant.

On a Tour; Getting to the Point

In no case does a docent tour take the place of, or compete with the museum signage or the self-guided tour. The docent tour is a way that a guide can help museum visitors look more closely at some of the art works in the museum. In contrast, visitors who rely solely on wall labels for their information often spend more time reading them than looking at the art. In some cases museum visitors read the signage *in place of* looking at the art. It has been estimated that the average time spent reading the signage is less than sixty seconds; the average time spent looking at the actual art work is approximately eight seconds.

The point of a docent-led tour is that the docent is standing in front of the original work. The visitor can slow down and listen to the tour guide while having time to admire, peruse, and think about the art work. The tour gives the visitor a chance to pause.

On the premise that less is more, the docent will often wait a few moments to give the group a chance to pay attention to particular features of the work. Exposure to the art is itself persuasive. On a tour, a docent will occasionally keep quiet. To quote Mark Rothko, "silence is so exact."

Some Distinguishing Features of Visitors

There are always certain museum visitors who are reliable, predictable and found in large numbers in any art museum. Docents look forward to these visitors. Some of the characteristics that typify this group are:

The Personal Browser: The term *Personal Browser* in a museum does not describe a way to access the web. Instead, the Browser is a person who is looking for a sensible, constrained reason for connecting to the art works rather than an emotive and subjective reason. This visitor may be extremely excited about the museum experience, but has such a deadpan expression that the docent will never know how much fun the Browser is having.

The Family Do-Gooder: This is a parent who does not care for art in the least, but feels that taking their children to an art museum is good for them; much as one might think that castor oil is good for the juvenile digestive tract. The children on the tour are prepared to feel a whack on their heads if any on the tour are not closely listening to the docent.

The Party Companion: The museum tour is like a party for this guest. The Party Companion usually brings many friends. At the end of the tour, since the tour was looked upon as part of the entertainment, everyone had a good time.

The Opinion-Filled Expert: This museum visitor feels that his knowledge will add a great deal to the tour experience. If the tour guide gives an open and congenial tour, the Opinion-Filled Expert will give numerous personal appraisals and remark upon most (if not all) of the artworks on the tour. The Opinion-Filled Expert will leave the tour satisfied that he/she has been of great assistance.

The Ardent Follower: This visitor is inspired by all the artworks in the museum. The Ardent Follower has visited many of the world's great museums. Now, as if on pilgrimage,

The Follower will take the docent tour to find the one work of art in the museum to which to pay homage. Unbeknownst to the docent, a small shrine to that one work might very well be constructed in the Follower's home. Look for The Ardent Follower to respectfully return to their particular piece many times. A small genuflection might be observed.

Linking/Bonding/Joining

The docent and the visitor might very well never again be in the same place at the same time. Fortuitously, their paths have crossed. What was heard was more than distant voices. The docent has earned the title "gate keeper." When there has been sustained communication which sparks long term interest in the museum and its collection, the docent's job has been fulfilled. This is the docent recompense. This is when the docent can go home contented and buoyed. Docents are visitor-centered people. They recharge themselves by plugging the museum visitor into the museum's collections. *Zap*....there goes another connection!

Let's Get Technical

Rules of the Museum Road

There is a technical side to public speaking. Many docents have read "how to" books on public speaking, taken classes in public speaking, and/or come from a public speaking background.

There are tricks of the trade that keep the docent-led tour from becoming sub-prime. The next time you take a docent-led tour, see if these simple and obvious rules are observed:

- The voice of the docent is at an optimal volume for the situation. Speaking softly is helpful when getting the attention of young students who are kinetic and clamoring. Speaking loudly is necessary in situations where the ambient noise level makes it clear that strong volume is the only way to be heard.
- There is occasional eye contact throughout the tour. Eye contact between guide and visitors leaves a pleasant impression. Conversely, frequent cold, hard stares suggest dominance. No visitor wants to walk away from a tour thinking that what was actually on the docent's mind was *veni, vidi, vici*.
- There are effective gestures by the tour guide to help affirm their statements. Gestures are always telling to others. Manic throwing of arms creates an image of a large, out-of-control Raggedy Ann/Andy doll. But hands and arms glued in place gives the impression of starched formality.
- "Speech fillers," which are superfluous sounds or words, are avoided. Effective public speakers won't use words or phrases such as the following: *"To be honest, like, I mean, um… you know."* **Whatever….**
- A well thought-out mission statement is delineated: this is a defining statement that will describe the premise of the tour.
- During the tour, talking points are used. Talking points are essential to support the tour's mission statement and identify the various art works included in the specific tour.
- The tour guide includes pieces of information that are points of fact or references that visitors are least expecting or are surprised to hear. These small

pieces of unusual or amusing knowledge generally delight the visitors and quickly help bond the docent to the group.

Practicing For Tours

There is no baseball game without a bat, there is no dinner party without plates and cutlery, and there is no tour without preparation. Waiting until the very last minute to go over touring plans is risky business. It is always too soon until it is too late: getting a tour organized in advance will keep the docent out of uncharted waters.

Practicing for tours is like any other skill-building activity: it is not meant to be casual, or occasional, or reserved for practice only when convenient. Without practice it is easy for the guide to look like a deer caught in the headlights in the middle of a tour. In museum-speak... non-practice for a tour is the equivalent of docent malpractice.

Caught In the Amber of Old Accomplishments

After giving a tour many times the docent must make the necessary changes to create a new way to present the information. Working up new tours is part of the job; though truth is timeless, docent talks reach statutes of limitations. In the docent ledger, to paraphrase Henry Miller, "there is no such thing as frozen assets." Thought is always given to lifting a tour above the level of comfortable mediocrity. Giving the same tour over and over again might feel as easy as pulling on an old sweater, but old sweaters become musty and their bouquet becomes difficult to mask.

The Message

It is quite likely that visitors will arrive at the museum with preconceived expectations about the art. No one comes with a blank slate mind. It is easy to have built-in personal judgments about art works. What distinguish the experiences on a guided tour are the opportunities visitors have to absorb and process new information.

Tours in art museums are based on a catch and release policy: the art works are there for the honored guests to discover and for which they are free to form their own opinions.

The Reasons Not to Compare

The message morphs into something resembling opinionated authority when the tone of a tour becomes a way to compare one art piece to another. Comparisons can lead to subjective opinions that are based on something other than the intrinsic significance of the works themselves.

Nor is the tour ever about the monetary value of the various artworks, though many a visitor will ask for estimates of their approximate worth. Thankfully, the curious visitors can be steered to the internet where any object in the collection of a public museum is commercialized in bold type with information not only about its auctionable value, but also about how to buy a print of any masterpiece in various sizes, giclee or non-giclee, framed or unframed.

Free to the Public: Trifle to Twinkies

Picture a shop that serves free samples of desserts. There are many sample items in its window; lemon meringue pie, crème brulee, chocolate éclairs, apple pie, classic cheesecake, blueberry cobbler, mango sorbet, angel food cake, ginger snaps, Swiss chocolates, jelly donuts and chocolate chip cookies. All the patron needs to do is to come into the diner and freely sample the hors d'oeuvre-sized portions of desserts. But there is a catch: the clients are seated at a table and the desserts are selected for them. The patrons taste the desserts that are offered. The waiter stands to the side as the guest is eating and describes each dessert, including its origins, its ingredients, the method of cooking and other salient information related to the sweet course.

Some of the desserts are items the customer has never tried. Some are old favorites. Each time the patron returns to the free sample shop, there are different desserts. The customers are free to decide which desserts they like best.

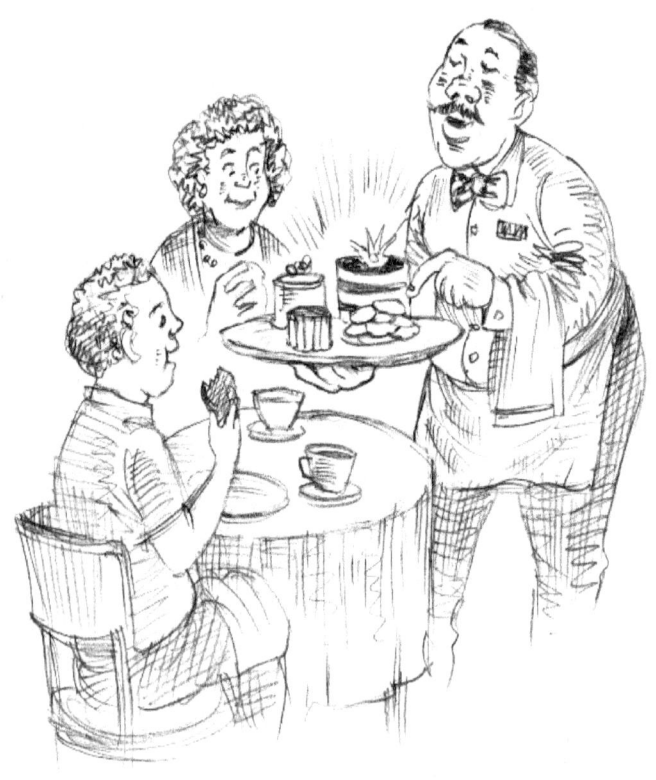

The dessert analogy holds true for an art museum. The museum exhibits are like an open buffet: the visitors are free to sample all the art works that are on display. The docent, acting as the waiter, has selected certain works to consider, describing the art and discussing any relevant information.

These descriptions are meant to enhance the enjoyment and expand the pleasure of the visitor. Into this mix, it would not be appropriate for the guide to compare the art works, any more than it would be suitable to rank the desserts, one above the other. The visitors might very well have a favorite, but on a tour, the visitor is asked to look at all the works.

Say What You Mean, Mean What You Say

A tour guide's statements can sound haughty and more than a little confusing. Any tour is best if there are no hidden, encoded meanings. Sometimes it might seem to the visitor as if there is a secret foreign language being used, when in fact it is the mother tongue applied in the manner of a specialist. Here is an example: *"The artist has explored angular notions of intricacy and monumentality; look at the asymmetry; look at the saturation."* The visitor is waiting for the guide to exhale: stringing words together in learned but coded sequences will do nothing to foster the visitor's understanding of the art works. And sadly, the magnificent building that was created to house a collection to strengthen connections with the public, now begins to look like the temple of boredom.

Moving Toward Expertise

The educated docent is all grown up, but not a bit stuffy as he or she presents the information. The tour guide is there to provide context and the tour is planned for the enjoyment and general education of the viewing public. The

73

tour will be targeted to a realistic level of comprehension, and in the process of the tour the visitor will begin to understand that, when it comes to appreciation, there is very little significant difference between him and the experts. The message to the visitor should be that the difference between specialist and non-specialist is not one of kind, but one of degree. As the visitors absorb their new touring experience, each in their own way, they will come away feeling that they are on the road to expertise.

Easy Does It

The tour draws attention to new views, but on the other hand, the substance of the tour should not be presented as the qualifying material for a Mensa exam. Information is usually comprehended in small increments. Not everyone absorbs information in a nanosecond and the process of learning is far from linear. If the tour guide takes on the Sisyphean task of becoming the all-knowing "headmaster/teacher," they will be seen as the person who is about to give the visitors a "Certified Art Test." What is accomplished is that the tour might very well be snatched from the jaws of victory and tossed into the jowls of defeat; not to mention that the touring public will be looking for the nearest broom closet in which to lock the guide.

Mind the Gaffe

The tour can be a wonderful wander or an agitated amble. It is stress and tension which gives people a feeling of unease, like nails on a chalkboard. If a docent forgets, stumbles or otherwise makes a mistake, no matter how noticeable the blunder, there always remains the possibility for a favorable outcome. The happy truth is that even small mistakes by the docent are usually taken lightly, or go unnoticed by the visitors. As with many things in life, humor is a tour guide's best friend and finding humor in failures is an even greater triumph than celebrating success. The tour that is filled with humility, fun and enthusiasm will be the tour that is warmly remembered.

Will the tour entice visitors to come to the museum more frequently? Of the sights that are necessary to see in person, the tour should have convinced the visitors that the museum is one of them. One satisfied museum visitor put it this way: "I don't think there is any substitute for going to an art museum...Some things are just inherently aesthetic; you need to be in their presence to understand them. Other things, it's not so necessary."

Touring While Senior

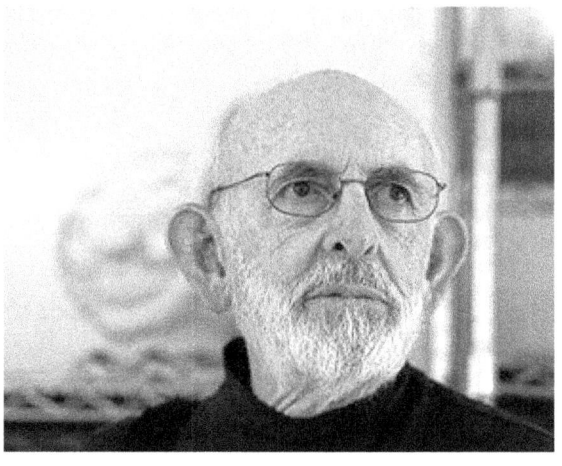

Persons of a Pensionable Age
Yes, it's true, we are getting older. And if you are among the chosen few who have lived your four score and ten (or more) you have probably done it all: gone to school, fallen

75

in love, diapered babies, shouldered heavy responsibilities, earned money, thought about reforming the world, lost weight, gained weight, taken your doctor's advice, ignored all advice, watched as technology moved more quickly than you, taken life too seriously, been shocked, lost loved ones, learned to be more amused than shocked, and have come to realize that being older can mean happier than being younger. As Oliver Wendell Holmes said, "To be seventy years young is sometimes far more cheerful and hopeful than to be forty years old."

The question now is the quality of one's life. What endeavor would you like to take on? Perhaps you are considering carving out a new niche or role for yourself. Does becoming a tour guide in your local art museum interest you? It is an excellent habitat for older humanity. You need not be concerned that if you enter a docent training program you will be the new kid on the block. You will be, but no one will mention it. The museums of this world put out the welcome mat for people like you. And if you take the step into the docent world, the chances of a bright future are ahead of you.

Caught between terror and ecstasy, I entered the museum offices, docent application in hand. My white hair bristled even more than usual and my left leg was acting up so that it was slightly spasming. Where this involuntary contraction came from, I'll never know. But now I appeared to have a minor limp as I shuffled up to the administrator's desk. After I told him that I was looking to enter the docent training program, I thought I sensed a smirk come over his face. I puffed up as I readied myself to become offended. He took my application in one hand and with his other, he pointed to a sign on the back wall of his office: "Old Dogs Can Learn New Tricks." He smiled and held out his hand for me to shake, as I am sure he could see the relief on my face.

It has been a long time since I experienced that frightening event. What I thought was going to be a fearful exposure of my frailties became an important touchstone moment. I have reevaluated my life since then and I know with the experience that has come with years of giving museum tours, that as long as I can admire art and share the love I have of art with others, I will be forever young.

Rose E.   Seattle, Washington

Facing the Limitations of Our Power and Control

As much as the older person might wish to ignore it, between the younger person and the older person, there will be generational differences. For instance, one's memory is not quite what it used to be and even though the older person is perfectly capable of learning new information, the arc for successfully committing that knowledge to memory takes a little longer. When going through the docent training class, the amount of material that a trainee receives and is expected to commit to memory sometimes feels like drinking water from a fire hose: there can be a giant fountain of facts coming your way.

For the anxious septuagenarian who is determined to "get it right" here is a pointer: for the forgivably forgetful there is always the occasional inked word on the palm of one's hand. Though this type of clue is probably unnecessary, it might console nervous seniors and give them the feeling of well-being that they need to complete their tour without anxiety. And there is the reassurance that there is little chance that any visitor will detect what looks like a few ink smudges on the skin. There is the almost one hundred percent guarantee that with so many tattoo wearers in this world, a "skin crib note" will surely go unnoticed.

As with so many other so-called "serious" items in life, it is best not to spend too much time worrying about an infrequent gaffe such as attributing a painting to the wrong artist. If attribution is occasionally ascribed to another artist, the world will not fall apart. A senior citizen will know to continue on their tour, finishing the job as narrator, presenter, host and (very occasionally inconstant) scholar.

Knees and Hips When In the Joint

While giving docent tours, the body as well as the mind will be strengthened. Yet, for the physically creaky, a little artful planning helps keep a tour within manageable proportions. Since no one wants to come home from a tour feeling ground and pounded, it is best to take a trial run of any new tour route. Walking through a tour before trying it out on the general public will ensure that joints are in military preparedness, ready and able to serve.

Since ease of movement is paramount, the older person is always looking for the most comfortable pair of shoes and the least restricting clothing. And with the wisdom that comes from a few years under the belt, there will be no attempt to dress to the nines. After all, it is docent work in an art museum; no one is getting married or buried.

In the Age of Aging: Visitor's Reactions

It is a rare occurrence, but there are times when an elderly docent might have to overcome an ageism barrier.

Ageism discrimination is usually unspoken and can be of such an inconsequential and insubstantial nature that it will be easy for the mature docent to overcome. In the process of dealing with the general public, coming across stereotyping of one type or another is probably inevitable. It will be up to the docent to show generosity of spirit and magnanimously go on with a great tour, exemplifying and validating the excellent contributions that an elderly tour guide can make.

While staying current on contemporary events and giving fun-filled informational tours, the docent will be able to turn around even the hardened cynic's mind. All art was once new, and all older docents were once young. What has been added as one matures are such characteristics as broader wisdom, understanding and knowledge. The visitor who at the start of a tour might have acted like a brute by subtly or not-so-subtly exhibited an age-based bias, by the end of the tour will have raised his hairy arm to give the elderly docent two opposable thumbs up.

Mind the Mind

Learning is not confined to childhood or the classroom but takes place throughout life and in a range of situations. Lifelong learning can be defined as the pursuit of knowledge for personal reasons. And lifelong learning is inevitable while working as a docent in an art museum. Mental sharpness is one of the most satisfying aspects of becoming a tour guide. Knowledge acquired about the history and aesthetics of art is extremely gratifying and as a tour guide, social interaction with the others who inhabit the museum is not only inescapable but enjoyable. The experience of being a tour guide enhances social inclusion, active citizenship and personal development. In this way this volunteer job becomes significant and worthwhile not only to the elderly docent but also to the community. In essence, the senior citizen docent becomes a community asset.

In the Next Chapter...

In the next chapter the tricks of the tour guide's trade will be explored. Get ready to laugh as we see how docent tips might fend off some museum problems.

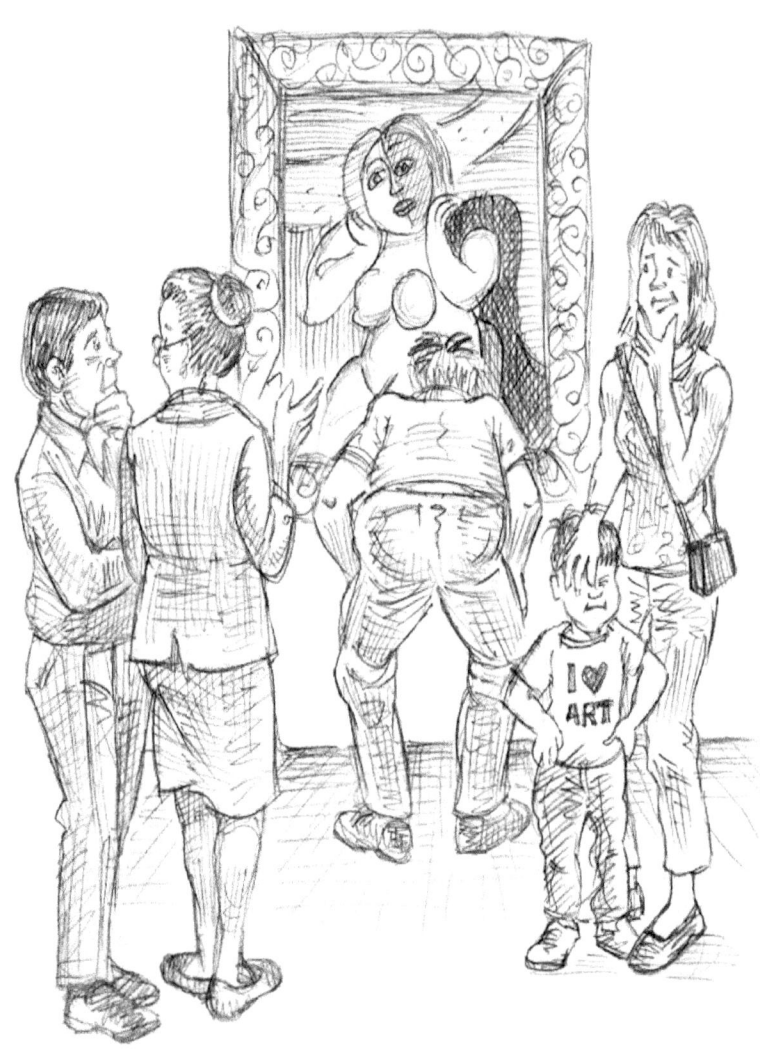

Chapter Five

When out on the touring floor: *"You will know more than you think you know, and…less than you want to know."*
Oscar Wilde

Tips for Touring Children and Adults

After you become a docent, or if you are a tour guide and would like to refresh your techniques, there may be a need to shine the light on ways to avoid the hassle, bring back the razzle, and polish up the dazzle.

Ready, Set, Go…Touring Adults

When launching a tour, the first order of business after the welcome is the docent's name, rank and touring subject. The tour actually begins when the guide asks the museum guests questions that will help to gauge the level of information and details to be given on the tour. The tour needs to be both intimate and formal, like the attitude of a welcoming host entertaining guests wearing hobnail boots on a glass floor.

Since it is difficult to adjust a tour in-progress, it is best to do collective bargaining with the visitors before you let the train out of the station. There might well be visitor conditions with respect to objects of interest or non-interest, problems with physical stamina, time-and-tribulation constraints, etc. Negotiations and agreements should be settled civilly and quickly at the beginning of the tour.

No two tours are ever the same: the guide must be adept at predicting the unpredictable. For those guides with a sporting sense, try to use the instincts of a football coach, the one who can play the field without a scorecard. Otherwise, the usual psychic abilities will do.

What Really Matters

If you program the following information into your internal GPS you will find that your helpfulness will increase tenfold.   Below are the most pragmatic and inescapable questions asked by the visitor:

Location of toilets/   Never underestimate the importance of bathroom sites;

Where the exits are located/ Sometimes a visitor is on-the-lamb;

Location and hours of the museum café/gift shop/ Cravings are ubiquitous;

Where a specific collection resides/ Well, as long as a visitor is here;

Information about the permanent artwork/ This is the fun part.

The museum exhibitions are not unimportant to the visitors, but the unvarnished truth is that real life comes before the theoretical. It is not that bubbles about ideal visits and perfect touring situations should be burst. But some visitors have travelled hours, days or weeks to reach their museum destination. They will need to know where the potty stops are, or their own bubbles might burst. Though most of the visitors will have, or are about to gain affection for the museum, they will still exhibit their human propensity to learn the lay of the land, mark their territory, and sniff out locations to forage. Dorothy Parker was almost right when she said: "all one needs is love and roughage." She forgot the part about a good art docent tour, but she got two out of three.

When I Say No, It Is Just a Manner of Speaking

The rules of the museum are always to be followed. But stating each and every rule at the beginning of a tour begins to make the docent sound like a governing authority issuing edicts. There are many rules that can be left unsaid, such as "do not urinate on the artworks." This is definitely an enforceable rule that, under no circumstances may be broken. Yet it is also one that is likely to be observed without a public declaration. To delineate all the rules before setting the tour in motion might make the visitors feel like the restrictions are so multitudinous and severe that the only actions left to freely observe must be obligatory.

Contents of the Tour/Putting Pieces Together

The gold standard is the tour that is "framed." A docent tour with a subject that has an overarching perspective to stitch the works together is most easily grasped. This might sound difficult, but it boils down to a process of assembling…if you can put together a jigsaw puzzle, you can gather your tour information into a comprehensible talk.

The Tour in the Aggregate, Not to Aggravate

The tour guide can be likened to a car with three gears. Some docents' gears are set in first and need revving up: *Shuffle off to Buffalo* is definitely twentieth century. Other guides are like race cars, very little slows them down. Science has shown that humans get the most benefit out of short bursts of moderate exercise. Always work on keeping the guests in a reasonable metabolic zone.

Pile on the Remedies

From time to time during the tour there is a need to give the visitors a break. All people, large and small, become weary and need to sit down occasionally. Expressions that show exhaustion are: bleary eyes rolling around in various directions within the eye sockets and shifting from one foot to another. In children this activity shows a need for a potty break or brain strain; in adults it might very well indicate strain in another portion of the anatomy. Older adults sometimes need to rest their rectitudes. Intermittently guiding the tour to strategic places where there is some sort of seating will engender untold gratitude from the multitudes. Strive for comfort as well as interesting, enjoyable tours and remember to give the visitors recovery time: visit artworks that have a bench in front of them.

Visible Clues

Tour guides are sometimes swayed by their own enthusiasm to give excessively long tours. The visitors have a life outside the museum. The docent should respect this and remember that at times it is out of politeness or convention that visitors do not protest an overly lengthy tour. The adage is: *use only one tank of gas per tour.* Just because you might come with an internal backup fuel tank doesn't necessarily mean the visitors will.

Clues for the oblivious tour guide that indicate the tour is going on too long: the visitor gets on a cell phone and orders pizza or another fast food take-out item. This will be prima facie evidence that it is time to suck-up your diaphragm, click your heels and wrap it up.

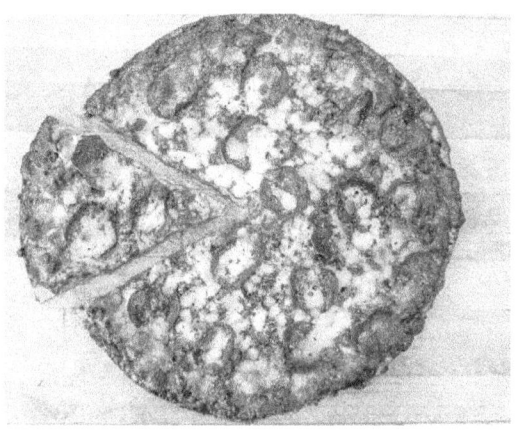

Distracted Walkers

There will be times when a large tour group will awkwardly traipse around bumping into themselves: at the same time one or two visitors will be squeezing to the front at the various stops to get a better look at the artworks. The docent must exhibit the skills of a croupier attempting to assist, distribute and locate the various guests so the chips will not fall where they may.

In Mediation Mode

There are times when the tour guide will need ombudsman-like abilities. On the tour it is the docent who represents the museum. Out on the floor, the guide is best situated to quickly investigate and resolve complaints. There are various reasons a person might become an at-risk tour visitor. If possible, try to catch this type of guest before they peel off from the group. If you keep your wits about you, their complaint might quickly be investigated, mediated and resolved. After you have solved their problem, try not to gloat at the fact that you have created one more satisfied customer.

Caution: Stop Logorrhea

There are museum guests who might wish to share an overabundance of information about what they know, going on and on about artworks they have seen. The kindly docent might allow such deluges to flow from the visitor's lips for time periods resembling The Great Flood. Other visitors may not wish to hear the person's life experiences, especially in scriptural length. If there is a dominant visitor ready to expostulate in blitzkrieg fashion, the docent must take action. To not intervene is an error of compassion and will affect the tour's quality for the other visitors. Inclusivity is always of prime importance on a tour. A helpful reminder to the unremitting talker might be that it is the provenance of the artworks that are of importance, and not that of the guests.

A Possible Non-Issue

There may come a time when it is obvious that a visitor is stealthily stalking you like a vengeful ex. This behavior may be more complimentary than criminal.
Your response should be:
A) Stop and ask the visitor to join the group;
B) Ask why they are loitering;

C) Find out why they are partially hiding around the corner.

It could easily be that the visitor is fascinated with your tour and was afraid of joining for fear of disrupting the others. Of course, you are most happy for all museum guests to hear every salient word.

If the visitor 1) doesn't answer you; 2) turns up the collar of their trench coat; and 3) slinks back into the gloom…look for your nearest escape hatch. Some museum windows are even large enough to allow the exit of a fully grown person.

Solutions Sometimes are in the Art

It is not unusual to have a group of touring adults with one or two intractable husbands in the ranks. The poor men were dragged kicking and screaming to the art museum and are now left on the docent's doormat with a problematic look on their face. This tip usually works: <u>nudes</u>. Most museums are littered with nudes in some form or another: nudes in paintings, nudes in sculptures, nudes in bas relief, and nudes in art photographs. Include some of these inanimate ladies on your tour. It is of little consequence for the culture-vulture wife if artistic nudes are discussed: after all, we are not thrashing out the merits of erotica. All in all, there is a good chance that the men's interest in art will perk up.

Getting Deep into the Weeds

The conclusion of a tour for adults does well when ended with a flourish: pick some favorite artwork to talk about that you know is popular. If you are planning to make a pitch for museum membership, the conclusion is the appropriate place to endeavor to persuade.

Answering questions from the visitors is important throughout the tour, but there needs to be special emphasis on encouraging visitor questions at the end of your talk. The visitor's questions will sometimes be cogent, specific and above your pay grade. Let's face it...it is possible that you won't have a clue as to what the answer is. At this point you can be honest with the guests about your ignorance. Or, to look like a tour guide with honorary medals, try the statement, "I am not allowed to reveal my sources." That remark always adds a bit of mystery to your ethos.

There are times when, at the end of your tour, you might feel drained, weary and you are thinking poorly. Resist the temptation to wrap up with trite, stale or commonplace remarks. Keep your motor running until the show is over, then you can rest. The rule is: don't make your conclusion the place where you got tired of thinking.

Ready, Set, Go.... *Touring Children*

Giving tours to children is quite a different matter from giving tours to adults. For one thing, the child is shorter and it helps to understand this perspective by kneeling down on the floor to the level of the children, to see what they see. The depth of the kneeling, of course, is in proportion to the age of the children. You will find in the case of very small children, it is a little like peering at the artwork while inside a gopher hole. While viewing the museum's art on the level of the very small child, you might try getting down on all fours, straining your neck and lifting your head.

This type of docent detective work is best accomplished in advance of the actual tour. If, on your mission, you are caught by a museum visitor in the prone position, rump up, in front of a piece of art, you will be thought of as an eccentric. There is always a slim possibility that you will have a chance to explain your strange behavior and be given a Hail Mary Pass. Trying to explain the same behavior when actually giving a tour to the students might put you in jeopardy of losing the respect of every child on the tour. It's your call.

Family/A basic social unit consisting of parents and their children

It is a good idea to take a measured assessment of the child's situation before giving tours to families with children. Below is a test question. Circle the correct answer:

A quiz:
Jack and Mary came to the museum with their five year old daughter and their eight year old son. Mary said they were interested in the historic art in the older section of the museum. It was a slow day and Docent Jane had time to concentrate on Jack and Mary. Since Jack and Mary voiced their desire to see the historic artworks, Docent Jane geared the tour to them. She had discussed the medieval works and was talking about the Renaissance pieces when: (What happened?)

a) **The eight year old son piped up and said he was studying Renaissance art in his class and proceeded to identify many of the works in that section of the museum;**

b) **The five year old daughter was so impressed with Docent Jane's erudite presentation that she said when she grew up she wanted to become an artist in the manner of Frans Hals;**

c) The two children were unruly the entire length of the tour, but Jack and Mary were well aware that their children were exceptional and were so enthralled with what was being said, they ignored their screaming, yelling children;

d) The two children fidgeted so much that Mary and Jack had to politely excuse themselves and took their two squirmy children to the museum's playroom.

The correct answers are, any from a) through c) if the children are in a precocious/gifted/genius program at their local Montessori School. Young children in this category will soon be advanced to university level and by the time they are in their early teens, will have earned a post-doctorate degree; but only if they learned to stop screaming when they didn't get their way.

Otherwise, if the parents and children are normal, d) is the correct answer. When giving a tour to families, the tour guide will focus the majority of time on addressing the children. This way, everyone is happy.

Who's Worried Now?

Dear Art Abby,

I am worried about my son. For years I have followed him around when we visit the museum.

At four years old the pictures that held my son's attention were ones that illustrated the stories he read in his picture books.

At seven years old what interested him were pictures of people who were moving in familiar poses…running, jumping, falling, sleeping, that sort of thing.

At ten years old my son liked to see pictures of heroes and bad guys or people who looked like monsters that scare in the night.

At thirteen years old he peered at historical portraits and thought it was interesting to find out how much a painting cost.

He is now sixteen and I find he has mysterious paths he has plotted within the museum that move him stealthily on missions he no longer shares with me.

As I follow my son, (always at a distance so he can't see me), I find that in the religious section he is inspecting only the Eve portion of the Adam and Eve paintings.

When he visits the mythological section he seems uninterested in the traditional legends, but he pays suspiciously close attention to the naked Venuses.

And when I secretly follow him into the vicinity of the nineteenth century paintings, he seems to me to be drooling in front of the harem scenes.

I am so worried. What is a mother to do?

Dear Worried Mother,

Be happy your very normal teenage son still likes going to the museum. My advice is to stop stalking him. He might learn a far more harmful lesson from your behavior than the one he is obviously enjoying when looking at the art works.

Art Abby

Things Can Get Prickly...Or, The Trials and Tribulations of Docent Lizzie

While introducing a classical painting to a tour group of teen-age girls, Docent Lizzie was startled to realize that a number of the girls on the tour had stayed behind at the last stop.

"What are they doing?" Docent Lizzie asked in the middle of expostulating to the remaining girls about the classical picture in front of them.

Several girls turned their heads to look in the direction of the strayed group. Giggling, one of the girls mumbled something about "Pump, squeeze and squirt."

Though Docent Lizzie was good-natured and usually thought the best of everyone, she immediately became suspicious of the cluster of girls who were keeping such a distance between themselves and the rest of the troop that they could easily be with an entirely different tour.

At the very moment Docent Lizzie was thinking this skeptical thought, one of the girls in the group who had wandered off took a syringe out of her purse and proceeded to slightly adjust her pant's waistline downward. Before Docent Lizzie had a chance to react; in plunged the needle. The group of stray girls surrounding the girl all looked on approvingly.

Docent Lizzie lunged toward the area where the shifty girls were standing. Just as she began to do so, a large hand grasped her shoulder and promptly stopped her. The hand was connected to the body of a passing teacher. The teacher quickly informed Docent Lizzie that the girl with the hypodermic needle had a doctor's prescription and that the class always tried to be supportive of her when the girl felt she needed to give herself an injection.

Docent Lizzie felt the pang of regret as she guiltily confessed to the teacher that she had thought the girls were colluding in some kind of drug deal.

"Pump, squeeze and squirt," the teacher chuckled. "It's code for supporting the only diabetic in our class."

Touring Teens or, I'd Rather be in Philadelphia

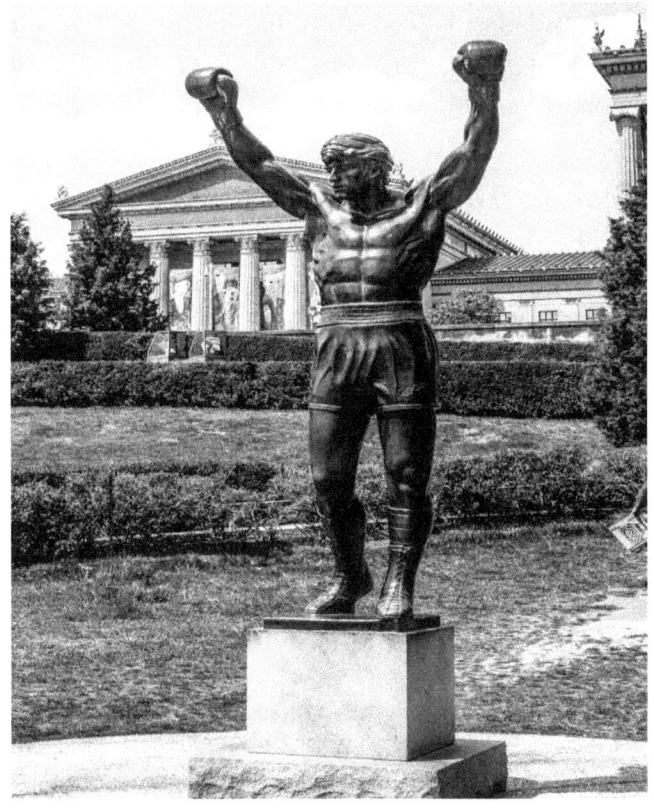

Philadelphia's Rocky

The teenager is a special organism capable of filling the docent with great hope and at the same time, great dread. The teenager is betwixt and between, and so may exhibit childhood displays of nonsense at one moment and the next moment demonstrate mature, insightful behavior. The docent will be challenged and should handle teens in the same manner one would handle any other challenge; with fear, loathing and apprehension.

At this point, to give new docents encouragement, it is helpful if they remember the words of Gustave Flaubert:

The most glorious moments in your life are not the so-called days of success, but rather those days when out of dejection and despair you feel the rise in you for a challenge to life, and the promise of future accomplishments.

How Cool Art Yo?

Along the same lines that Gus is proposing, you need to remember to pull yourself up to the challenges of the day, keep your equanimity and not allow the teens to whom you are about to give a tour, to get you down. When urban, hip teenagers enter the museum, why not start out with a small ditty, perhaps accompanied by a little dance? Here are rap lyrics that you can easily make your own:

Jest Call the Museum "*Moosie*"
I say yo, I can rap, an' I can play it cool;
An' I won't allow no nap, just because you ain't in school.
We gonna see color, like the color red;
An' this color yo gonna remember 'till yo is dead.
It's like this my friends, an' I do mean friends;
Yo gonna like these pictures more than ridin' in a Benz.

So if yo mama leaves yo an yo don't know where to go;
Just cruise on down to *moosie* fo the next museum show.
We gonna take real care, to show yo some good stuff;
An' yo can count on somethin' other than jest the ol' dead puff.
So get up! Get down! Get on with this here guide;
I gonna sho yo things that'll put jammin' in yo stride.

How Appealing Can You Make It?

Of course, there are students who may be difficult to reach for reasons that defy your technological ability. These are the students who, disguised as ordinary young humans, can fix their grandmother's computer in a nanosecond or tell their dad how to create a new database which will revolutionize his business. Unfortunately, when they enter the museum, these teenagers are still involved in their state-of-the-art technology. They are easy to spot because their eyes are following their fingers and thumbs as they scan, hunt and peck at their iPads, Smart Phones, and other newer technologically advanced devices that will surely be invented, available, and wildly popular about three weeks after this book is published.

You will not be able to count on the transformative powers of the artworks in the museum unless you create an interest greater than the lure of their electronic equipment. Some museums have rules that electronic devices are not allowed to be used when on a tour. This is a wise policy. However, cyber security is, like all other types of enforcement aimed at teenagers, not always easily enforced.

It might be best to rebrand your tour to whet the appetites of the touring teenage techies. For instance, if you are standing in front of a classical painting of Dido and Aeneas, describe the painting as a "red hot" lover's story. The teenager's eyes might look up for an instance from their plastic, rectangular vision of life. This is your chance to catch the teens and reel them into the narrative.

The Virtual World and the Art

Try a narrative calculated to frustrate the teenage techno nerd's interest in hand-held electronics. Since most of these teenagers are hooked on video games, you could try the maneuver of presenting the art itself as a video game. Be as provocative as possible. Here is an example:

Dido and Aeneas, the Video Game

In the world of the Trojans, death and misfortune constantly haunt them on their long journey back to Italy. Aeneas is the captain of the Trojan ship and he has made the Goddess Juno really angry at him. Juno has superhuman strength and is creating havoc on the high seas. The Goddess Juno keeps sending problems their way, big time. Blood and destruction reign when the Harpies attack the Trojans. The Harpies, who are ravenous, filthy monsters with heads of women, bodies of birds and sets of wings that make them faster and cooler than drones, swoop down and pull off great chunks of Trojan flesh. Many Trojan soldiers die fighting off these creatures. It takes a whole arsenal of arrows to get the Harpies to back off. When Aeneas and his soldiers finally get on course to head for Italy again, the super-goddess Juno decides to send a huge, terrifying storm their way. POW! They are slammed onto a coast on the banks of a big city. The big city is ruled by a beautiful-looking gal named Dido. Dido may be a beauty and a big-shot, but she falls, lickety-split for the good-looking Aeneas. Aeneas isn't in love with Dido, but the tricky Goddess Juno casts a spell over Aeneas. So Dido and Aeneas get together. Dido is happy because she thinks she has married Aeneas. Where did she get such a messed-up idea? Finally, another God tells Aeneas to get the heck out of that city and ditch his girlfriend Dido. Aeneas says, "Okay Boss," and tells his men to get on the ship and split. The Trojans start sailing back to Italy. Dido is furious and heartbroken, so she does two things: 1) she puts an enormous curse on Aeneas and his Trojans; and 2) she kills herself.

For the video/picture: As one of the gods/goddesses looking down on all this drama, you travel with Aeneas and his Trojans and try to fend off Dido's curse and Juno's anger. You've got some rough sailing ahead of you.

A Touch of Seriousness

All tours need to be nuanced; sometimes there is only a fine distinction in the amount of gradation. At other times the degree is quite palpable. Nowhere is there a more obvious need for scaling the tour talk to the level of the visitor than in giving tours to children. And nowhere do you have a better chance to persuade and influence for the good of the museum and for art in general, than with the willing minds of the children. Students will consume and digest what you are telling them long after they leave the museum. Alas, you may never know the extent of your influence. The students who come into the museum may look ordinary, but if you see all of them as extraordinary, you will be doing them and the world of art a great service. Though the period of time you are with the children is brief, the potential you have for touching the youth of this world and accomplishing something life altering with your talk is very great.

May the force be with you.

In the Next Chapter...

Coming up, the world of contemporary art will be parsed, discussed and analyzed. Also looked at, because of its contemporary nature, will be the new world of digitization.

If you have ever had to explain to a friend or partner why you like those red spots on an all-white background, and had your viewer tell you they could have done a better job while shaving in the bathroom, then the next chapter is for you; abstract for the abject.

Chapter Six

Abandon All Hope, Ye Who Enter Here
Dante Alighieri

Contemporary Art: Making the Case

Art Can Be Messy

Is there any difference between modern art and contemporary art? In a nutshell, the answer is "yes." Classifications in the history of art can be vague and dispensation is normally given if the words "modern" or "contemporary" are substituted one for another. Attempting to identify the cutoff date and distinctions between modern and contemporary art can feel like jumping from a reverse bungee. Taking survey courses in modern and contemporary art won't help: the precise dates and details vary from one course and textbook to the next. The docent might be asked, "What is the difference between modern art and contemporary art?" Like Hamlet, the docent's explanation might quaver with the sound of damaged ambivalence.

To help keep the level of confusion at a minimum, there is a simple-minded way to remember the definition of "contemporary:" contemporary, as it pertains to art, means contemporary to *us*. Even with this simplified version there is some uncertainty: if you are 101 years old and are lively enough to be reading this chapter and are interested in becoming a docent, within your lifetime there will be a certain amount of coincidental overlapping between "contemporary" and "modern" art. (As an aside, I send you an enthusiastic salute and a sincere congrats to any person reading this who is over the age of 95. Carpe Diem!)

"Modern" art includes the Impressionists and all the art movements that were generated by the original nineteenth century Paris artist's group and whose art movements end in "-ism." Around the middle of the twentieth century, art critics and art historians decided that the *modern* art movement had ended and they put the era to bed by using the term "postmodern" for the artwork coming after that time period. Will there be a "post contemporary" historical period? In a way, we are in it. Stay tuned.

Nonbinding Definition

This simple summation of the significant differences between modern and contemporary art is just shorthand. It is not meant to be a substitute for months and years of study, should you choose to devote your valuable time learning the precise and accurate distinctions.

Exchanging and Interchanging

There is a way in which the terms "contemporary" and "modern" are interchangeable; a way which may be more, or perhaps less, confusing. For the purposes of this chapter, the word "modern" will be used generically from time to time as an overarching term to include contemporary art. There is precedent for this: notice that such a prestigious institution as the Museum of Modern Art in New York uses the term "modern" in their name, yet they frequently exhibit works that are "contemporary."

The Top of the Popularity Charts

There is no getting around the popularity of modern and contemporary art in America.

- Of the top twenty museums in terms of attendance in the United States, five are dedicated solely to exhibiting modern art;
- The total annual attendance in 2011 for the top five modern art museums in the United States was almost six million attendees;
- Of the top twenty American museums ranked for number of people attending, several modern art museums make that list: New York's *Museum of Modern Art* with a ranking of third; *The Guggenheim Museum* in New York with a ranking of ninth; and the *San Francisco Museum of Modern Art* with a ranking of thirteenth.

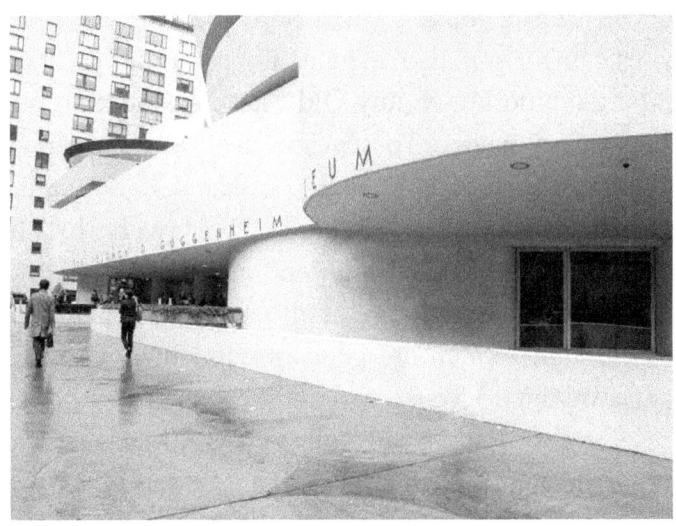

The Guggenheim Museum, New York City

Old and Masterly

Though there is wide approval of modern art and artists and they receive their share of accolades, there remains a paradox. Nowhere is President Lincoln's admonition about not being able to please all the people all the time more true than with the public's contradictory, even schizophrenic reception of modern and contemporary art. The most obvious point is that there are always the collections of the Old Masters to pit and compare with the artists of modern times. The Old Masters are primarily European painters who (1) worked before 1800; (2) when they were young, were trained in their craft by master artists; (3) were members of an artist's guild; (4) many times had entire schools where other artists were trained under their supervision.

Some of the Old Masters have become modern day headliners. Their works are legendary and the regard the public has for them is enormous. There is no doubt about the superlative skills and talents of the Old Masters.

Old Master works which are broadly recognized and highly esteemed are also a valuable commodity. For one thing, there are no longer any Old Masters around to produce more master art works. To seal the deal on their reputation, their popularity has been assured through the commercialization and publicity of their work by the art trading auction houses and high-end art galleries. People of wealth buy the works not only for enjoyment but as marketable items which are good investments. Too, there is status in owning Old Master works; it can be a way of keeping score. Because of this, the inventory of Old Master works has become associated with sale prices far too heady for most of today's museums.

Follow the Money

This is not to say that the same global influences that drive sales in other art markets are not also at work in the field of modern art. Modern day artists negotiate between the demands of artistic integrity and those of the market place. Numerous modern and contemporary works are auctioned whose prices are out of reach for most American museums.

For comparisons, the estimated value of the *Mona Lisa*, adjusted for 2012 dollars, is $768 million. In recent times, the highest price paid for a "modern" artist's painting was the sale of a work by Cezanne bought by the Royal Family of Qatar in 2011 for $267 million. And for an example of contemporary art, a painting by Francis Bacon created in 1976, was bought by a celebrity owner in 2008 for $86.3 million.

Masterworks of any era go up for sale very rarely and their prices will continue to appreciate. If you are interested in purchasing one, better start putting your pennies in your piggy bank now.

The Ephemeral Nature of Opinion

Despite the popularity of modern art, the reason why this chapter is dedicated to contemporary art is because there are times when giving a tour of contemporary art can be a hard sell. After all, Old Masters' works were predicated on skilled technical drawing and are usually representational scenes easily comprehended. The art of today is no longer frozen in a kind of orthodoxy of convention. Present day artists use all types of materials, techniques, devices and surfaces to get their message across…everything from digital images to natural pigments on cave walls.

How art transformed into its present modernity is taken up in voluminous detail in other books. Suffice it to say, the artists of modern and contemporary art have attempted to avoid working in the same vein as the artists of the past because that art eventually became overused to the point of losing its original meaning and effect.

The Same Old Story

Still, the art of today is similar to all art: it is a reflection of the times and values of the men and women who create it. No one creates in a vacuum or solely on their own terms. And because artists are creatures of their era, they are documenting the history of their time with their art. Modern artists have stepped outside the boundaries of past traditions and trust their inner visions; they experiment, innovate, and use the images and objects of their everyday world as their subjects.

What can confound the viewer is that the category of art forms that today's artwork can take is innumerable. Some contemporary art looks like Merlin the Magician pulled it out of a hat. Other artworks look like giant Chia pets. There is often little in common between one art grouping and another except their contradictory uniqueness.

There is Life/There is Art/ There is Art Lingo

To add to the perplexing amount of new ways to look at twentieth and twenty-first century art is the fact that there is now a whole new language with which to discuss it. Modern art has its own vocabulary, famous names, and distinguishing vernacular: the length of the list of new words specific to modern art is as long as the Torah. Artists whose names are unfamiliar in one household have earth-shaking reputations in another. All of a sudden it is possible to be so overwhelmed with the shock of the new that getting a grasp on it seems like Mission Impossible.

Here is a little test to see how you are keeping up:

Which is an actual word that describes a contemporary art movement?

(a)   Roochus
(b)   Fluxus
(c)   Lauditus

The answer is (b). Fluxus, much as it might sound like a word associated with potty training your toddler, is an international art movement. If you already knew that, why are you reading this book?

Select the name of an actual artist (recently deceased) who is world-renowned:

(a) John Deatorani
(b) David Zack
(c) Ivan the Terrible

The answer is (b), the famous mail artist David Zack. "Got Mail?" You knew that one too, didn't you?

Channel Your Inner Andy Warhol

On the tour, you will not always meet the proverbial reasonable visitor. The contemporary work might be popular with some visitors and an odious creation to others. Giving tours in the contemporary art section isn't always a slam dunk; which is to say, it is not always a post modernist paradise out there on the museum floor. There are visitors who are traditionalist and who mistakenly wander afield from their comfort zone and end up taking a tour of contemporary art.

To these visitors it might look like the docent is there to blow the whistle on conventional values. To the docent it may feel like there is a Sword of Damocles hanging somewhere in the gallery and imminent peril awaits.

Small Reasons that Irritate

One obvious problem that needs to be cleared up as soon as possible is that everything connected to modern and contemporary art is sometimes seen as elitist. There are various reasons for this opinion. When visitors, unaccustomed to a modern museum, come into the building for the first time there can be an overload of culture. Many contemporary museums are so imposing in their architectural grandeur that they give the impression that they are the kind of edifices that God would have built, if he had the money.

The modern art itself can look as if its techniques and intentions are untethered by convention or legacy. What the docent needs to remember is that the way in which the tour is presented could be a game changer for the unenthusiastic visitor.

There needs to be recognition by the docent that nothing is unassailable: visitor discussion and exchange about the artwork should be of paramount importance throughout the tour. But the point might need to be made that no one is asking the visitor to adopt new values and no one is attacking the visitor's moral authority.

New but Lofty Aspirations

Instead, the contemporary work is presented as the artists' earnest attempts to present new and authentic ways of looking at art. The artwork is a bona fide offer for us to expand our minds: there is no gain in coming into a contemporary art exhibit only to spend the time listening to the echoes in one's mind of ideologies of anti-modernism.

Nevertheless, when looking at the world of contemporary art, it may seem to some visitors like a cold and mysterious landscape. Originality might not breed contempt, but it may engender a series of emotional responses from the visitor different from the feelings that are elicited by pretty pictures. The reluctant visitor might be yearning to see their favorite traditional painting of an idealized nude in an idyllic landscape.

It Is Not The Red Zone

The visitors who are threatened by provocative, contemporary and previously unfamiliar art are frequently people who feel comfortable knowing their precise place in the cosmos. Following this logic it is understandable that they take the stand of righteous indignation: what they see in contemporary art is an attack on the changelessness of conventional values. Listening politely to a visitor's harsh opinions with acceptance will frequently weaken their criticisms and parenthetically present the artworks as versions of a different way to look at reality. The more slowly and carefully the tour is presented, the more likely the visitor will be able to see the multiple perspectives in the contemporary creations.

Passing Muster

Many times the work can be presented playfully. Some contemporary art is infused with irony and undercuts itself. At other times, the artwork is not a commentary on anything, it is just a story: perhaps it is a story that might momentarily destabilize accepted perceptions and tastes, but it remains chimerical in nature.

The viewer critical of creations of dystopian fantasy could be reminded that such art is not a novel invention, the artists of old presented similar narratives. Certainly there is an altered view in works by Hieronymus Bosch. There was even trouble in the pleasure dome of Xanadu.

Having a set of core questions to ask the visitors throughout the tour will establish an environment of civility. Agreeing that there is no appropriate emotional response to how the works should be interpreted will also assuage their consternation.

The more considered way in which each artwork is discussed, the more time the visitor will have to puzzle over each piece of art. This way, the tour can be broken down and fed in therapeutic doses. Small bits of information will draw the visitors into new ways to digest the art.

All aspects of the work warrant our attention. With contemporary paintings, for instance, many elements can be emphasized: the works are frequently very large and unframed; some of the paintings take on an entirely new form when there is no underlying drawing; photorealism is ultra-real and looks more authentic than a photograph. These are all observations where dialog can be exchanged.

Good News

When standing in front of a piece of visually equivocal art, even the most receptive of visitors in the contemporary section might ask one of these two questions:

"What is it?"

"What does it mean?"

The title of the art work may or may not be helpful. Sometimes the title is so ambiguous that a clear-cut interpretation is not possible. Other times the title will not identify the content of the piece and simply say "Untitled No. 3," etc. The good news is that each person is free to decide what the work is and what it means. Everyone is a citizen of an art museum and each citizen has a right to interpret the contemporary works in the manner that makes the works more accessible to them. This alone can initiate an interesting discussion.

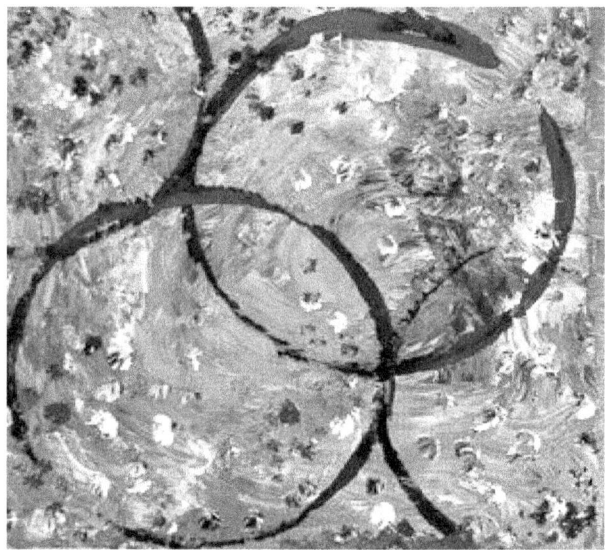

Form, line, color and abstract

It's Not Always Dialing For Dollars

There are times when a visitor's cultural viewpoint is rigidly fixed and no amount of skillfulness on the part of the tour guide will budge their personal pre-set opinions. If this is the case, it is their loss, not yours. If you are at a pay phone and you need to call numerous people, you wouldn't use all your change on the one reluctant person at the other end of the line who doesn't want to listen. You just carry on and contact all those people who are willing to hear what you have to say.

When is it Easier to Give a Tour to Children?

For museum visitors, the new, improved models come in the form of children; yes, the ones who don't think "hip-hop" has to do with a bunny's gait. Young people have far less interest in censorship. Also, there are fewer sacred cows grazing in the head of a child. Liberated from conscious presumption, the child is an easier customer when browsing through the contemporary art exhibits. Students are used to being educated in their school classes so when looking at contemporary art, what they see is not a work which does not conform to controlled prescriptions, but simply the art itself. The experience of giving a tour to children can be quite refreshing after foraging in the dry bones of a group of critical adults and not finding fresh water.

A Special Perk for the Tour Guide

Giving tours in a museum which holds a large number of contemporary pieces sometimes means that the docent will be hanging out in a place inhabited by artists. Though some contemporary artists will turn out to be one trick wonders, there will be other artists whose works will be lauded and applauded long after this century has ended. By viewing tomorrow's famous artworks and possibly meeting the artists who created them, the docent will have a chance to encounter history in the making

Contemporary artists are interesting specimens in their own right: some have reckless energy with little concern for convention or public reaction; others are enmeshed in appropriate audience responses and acceptance. The attitudes and personalities of artists run the gamut. There are artists who are introverted and may be shy or broody by temperament. The ironic contradiction is that though the birth of a work is a private and personal experience, it must be shared with others to be successful. Most artists whose works end up in museum collections will connect in some way with the museum that displays their works. It may be that the docent will be there when that connection takes place.

An Apparatus for the Ears: Auditory Sensations

Audio A- Go- Go

For a visitor who wants the Holy Grail, that is, a tour which is given from a curatorial or art museum expert's point of view, an audio tour will be sufficiently lengthy (many are over sixty minutes long) and erudite to satisfy any museum guest's discriminating taste. The scripted audio tour has the distinction of having been vetted and branded by authorities at the museum. Unlike the shared docent tour, there is very little possibility of slip-ups or misinformation in an audio tour.

The electronic revolution in art museums can be traced to the audio tour. The earliest tape recorders were patented in 1886; it took a few decades more for art museums to start using them as technological apparatuses for touring. Today, an audio tour provides many kinds of possibilities for a self-guided tour: there are Podcasts which can be downloaded onto mobile devises; there are scripted tours which can be streamed via cell phone; there are audio wands easily rented from the museum. Future electronic possibilities abound.

There are many advantages to an audio tour: the visitor can stop and start the tour at their leisure; there is no feeling of unease if the visitor would like to walk away and end the tour without completion; audio tours are always available, tour guides are not.

Yet there are also disadvantages to audio tours: there will be no possibility of a question and answer session (in the galleries dealing with contemporary art, this can be a vexing problem for the visitor), and the interactions are strictly between the visitor, the automated voice and the art work. This type of experience blurs the line between tour and techno experience. Much like watching television, even when the audio tour is simultaneously set on the same channel as other visitors, the experience is an isolated one. With a push of a button, mutual friends can be in synchrony on their audio tour but shared interactions are difficult.

Who or What Will Give The Tour?

Whether in the contemporary art section or other galleries, there will always be museum guests who are ready to walk, talk and rumble…enjoying an immediate experience with a tour guide in whose presence they can feel direct contact with the museum's artwork. For these visitors there is no substitute for the human touch. For many visitors there will never be a question as to whether to choose the hand held, ear-to-machine touring model, or the friendly, welcoming human model waiting to share a tour with them.

No More Cranking the Telephone

Museums offer a multitude of ways to get involved with their collections and special exhibits. Audio tours are one such way. But wait, there are virtual universes out there which make audio tours as passé as your friendly local telephone operator.

The Virtual World and the Docent

Sometimes it is best to embrace new ways to approach tours. This is especially true while working in the contemporary art section when, rather than acceptance or even rancorous argument from the visitors, the docent is greeted by a yawn of silence. Taking advantage of the new potentials that advanced technologies offer, the docent can use cyberspace and the electronic environment to energize the narratives of contemporary art.

Expertise/ Not Ill At Ease

Cognitive participation by the visitors is necessary for the tour: if no audible sound is heard from the group, and there is not a practical way to find a pulse, incorporating a virtual tour within the tour commentary may be a way to ensure that there are still heartbeats out there.

The advanced specialist in computer knowledge might well become the docent of the future. However, most of what is technologically possible to include in a docent tour is not intuitive. When used by a tour guide for instance, touch screen tablets can answer essential, off-the-cuff questions from the visitors in a quick and easy manner. But this is only the case if a docent is familiar with how to gain access, read quickly, and extemporize with no advance preparation. Electronic support can enrich a tour or, if there is only vague acquaintance with how to navigate the technology, could lead to a small but embarrassing calamity.

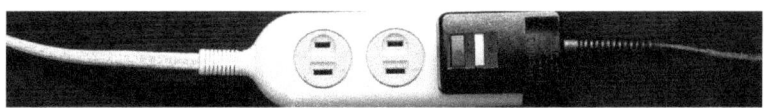

The Digital Museum Where You May Blog, You May Tweet

It is a new world and "digitization" is its name. With a blending of technology and art, the museums of today have many ways to connect to the virtual world. The most obvious is the web, both by making museum collections more accessible, and by creating web advertising to encourage live visits and online sales for the museum gift shops.

Museums are also using thousands of digital displays to connect with the visiting public. Updated museums may have touch screens loaded with interactive features that can be downloaded onto the visitor's electronic devices. Instead of walking around with a catalog, the visitor might use an electronic tablet to create personal lists of favorites or use an app that displays not only the image of the artwork, but a photo of how the artwork might look in various settings.

A paradox of the new paradigm is that a visitor may be physically present in the museum, but by connecting with the museum's app or web page, will also be a digital visitor. Through the electronic medium, visitors can generate their own tour which takes advantage of the artworks that are of primary interest to them: they can look up information in the museum library's app to supplement their tour; they can create their own pre-planned trails and work up museum maps.

The only thing left for the museum maintenance staff to do is to remember to turn on the equipment each day.

For a museum docent, the hope is, once you have mastered the touch screen tablet, your electronic mobility will allow you to not only deliver an improved tour but for the visitor's convenience, give updated weather and traffic reports as well.

Is Anthropomorphic All There Is?

So far the discussion has been limited to human docents and their experiences and purposes in the world of art museums. But there is a way in which this discussion is so last-century. New forms of docents may be coming: look for them soon on the grid.

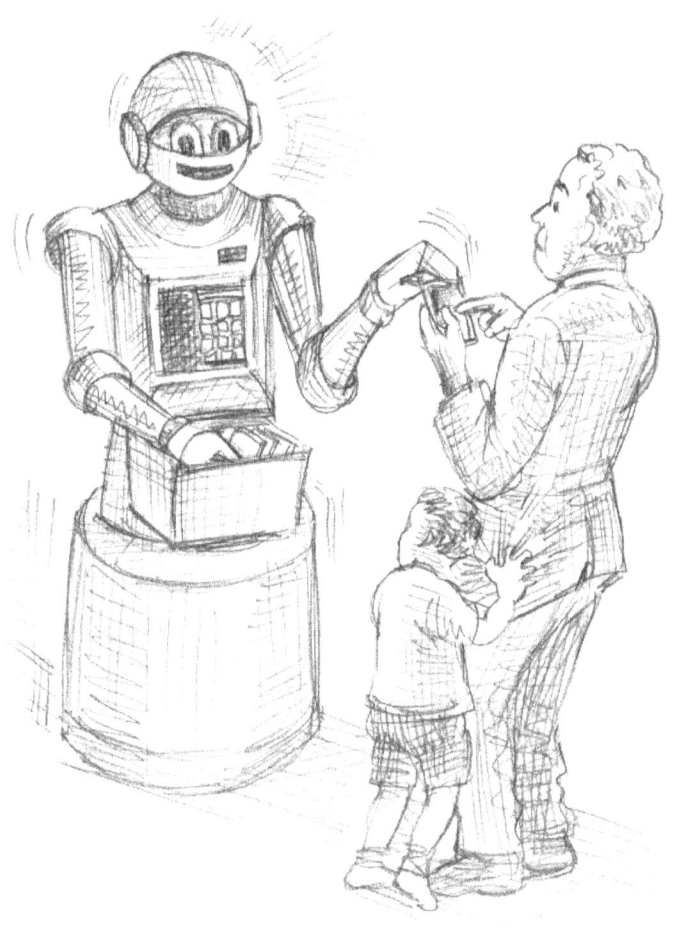

To rejuvenate the Old World human archetype, a cyberdocent robot has been proposed, one in which the functionality carries on human docent tasks, but without forgetfulness, substandard dress, or time-off. Behind this concept is more than a Rube Goldberg-type invention. The computer science geniuses who have proposed this clever artifice may even now be preparing to make human docents redundant. All that is needed is a widget here and a bolt there and the *interactive museum tour-guide robot* will be glided out, ready to automate and replace Homo Sapiens; robots who give perfectly guided, accommodating, factual tours presented in a cheerful, disembodied voice.

A Jaunty New Perspective

The techniques of the cyberdocent robot could give contemporary art a nifty new spin. When the *museum tour-guide robot* demonstration model was hauled out in 1997, the results were astonishing: besides smoothly navigating in a crowded museum, the robot increased the museum's attendance by over fifty percent. In addition to being able to seamlessly put a tour together in one billionth of a second, these human docent proxies will undoubtedly be able to read the visitor's minds, do body scans, and figure out how to impress upon the visitor the principles and elements of art, all within the limitations of a forty-five minute tour. Needless to say, the art of persuasion is what will be their greatest virtuosity. And rather than a little love, all the *interactive museum tour-guide robot* will need is a recharging station. The new, improved, prototype, stand-in docent may be out there today.

Oh cyberdocent robot, in which tours are you embedded? Imagine the possibilities!

In the Next Chapter...

When the electronic world is put aside, the docent will be interacting with the more commonplace, but many times more complex humans who are attached to the museum. In the next chapter we will be discussing some of the wide variety of relations possible in museums.

Chapter Seven

Friendship is a Sheltering Tree…
Samuel Taylor Coleridge

Building Relationships/Extra Curricular Activities

Bonding With More Than A Building

When asked why he robbed banks, Willie Sutton remarked, "That's where the money is." The same can be said of why we spend great chunks of time in an art museum: that's where the art is. But the truth be told, there are many other things that can be gained by spending time in the museum. Art museums are laboratories for social experimentation. For the person who becomes an art museum tour guide, the social context is broad and complex. There is always the obvious contact with the visitors. Since the past is foreign country, there is a continuous need for tour guides to discuss the works of art with the visitors. For the docent, the visible expressions of interest and gratitude from the visitors make for an enriching social experience and give a sense of purpose.

Also, if you stay long enough, you will inevitably discover a network of friends within the cadre of museum volunteers who share many of your same interests. There is a good possibility that you will find personal relationships that will last a lifetime.

Thoroughly Modern Millie

Art museums make a constant effort to stay ahead of the curve: this means the tour guide is swimming in the same Petri dish with people who are aware of the latest creative ideas, thoughts, and trends. You can be confident that when you are in conversation with these accomplished people you are drinking from the fountain of source material. Personal contacts between the individual docent and members of the art community can awaken change and conversion: the novel seems more practical; flexibility feels right. The very manner in which you approach viewing art may change. The feeling is like floating on a rising tide.

The journey often leads to progress in other directions of one's life. Ask any docent: being a guide in an art museum is an exhilarating and socially involved pursuit.

Attention to the Details

When first arriving in a docent study class, the experience can feel like going into another dimension. It is not just that the interior of the buildings are art-filled spaces beckoning you to see each piece with new eyes. There is a way in which the study and introduction of information, the discovery of new approaches, and the fresh and recent relationships you forge at the museum, initiates passage into new alternatives.

The collegiate involvement is rigorous and has a tendency to create fast friendships with the other team members in your learning group. Working together and sharing information encourages resiliency and buffers setbacks. The scholastic environment might include: the time spent in class, the materials to be read, the information to be remembered and the working out of practical approaches to touring. This exposure to the formal aspects of docent requirements might exceed your expectations. The motto of the Peace Corps could apply to docents: "The Toughest Job You'll Ever Love."

Tributes to Change

A person's experiences are unique, there are no people who are carbon copies of one another and each person's personal stories are original. But there are a few stories that are included in this chapter that symbolize the authentic transformation that might occur in art museums when having close encounters of the art kind.

Enlightenment in the City; A Story

We met in a restaurant; my restaurant to be exact. We were both busy people. Bob was working as a corporate attorney in New York and had always liked to kick- back after work and enjoy a good dinner. I owned several restaurants at the time and was looking for a partner with whom I could share my personal life. When we moved in together, a great deal of what Bob and I had in common centered on food.

As time went by I decided to get out of the restaurateur rat race and sold all three of my lucrative businesses. By that time my partner Bob and I had taken up another hobby that kept us bonded; working out together in the gym. We attempted to remain close, even though his work kept him away from the apartment for long hours and I was left to my own devices.

I had always dabbled in painting and drawing landscapes and still lifes; now I started to inhabit the art museum. Using the museum's masterworks as my models, I became engrossed in sketching. The more the museum became a place for my daytime respite, the more I became interested in the content of the talks given by the tour guides. Finally I told Bob that I was applying to train as an art museum docent.

Bob was less than enthused. His interests outside work were limited to restaurant hopping and going to the gym.

We had several arguments about my new-found interest in art and the arguments were especially severe regarding the large blocks of time I needed to complete my docent trainee studies.

Being a "bottom line" kind-of-guy, Bob couldn't see the benefit in volunteer work; to him it seemed like a giant Bolshevik plot. He specifically denounced docent work in an art museum saying, "It's like selling broccoli."

Even though sometimes Bob made me feel I was the living embodiment of Milton's idea of "voluntary humiliation," I continued on with my studies and worked diligently. The studies were arduous, but the research was always satisfying to me.

As time went by, Bob accompanied me to some of the museum sponsored social affairs and lectures. At these events he always seemed unimpressed and dyspeptic. His attitude toward my new found pursuit seemed to me like a refutation of our relationship.

One day he had an important social engagement where he needed me to attend. He was on the corporate ladder to make partner and his goal was to impress the two senior attorneys who headed his firm. We picked them up by taxi and took them to a top-of-the-line eatery. Being a gourmet, Bob knew how to impress, ordering just the right wine and entrees. Afterwards, in the anteroom when we were waiting for a cab, one of the senior partners became interested in a large painting on the wall. It was a contemporary piece painted by a relatively obscure artist, but an artist who was represented in the museum in which I was a docent.

I was ready to step in and identify the painter and say a few words about his style and the composition and history of the work, but as it turned out, I didn't have to. Bob-the-unimpressed-in-all-things-art winked in my direction and said, "I'll call you if I need you."

He started off by talking about the painter, saying, "It is difficult to say that one of his pieces is representative; it would be better to see a larger body of his work for comparison." Then his discussion led him to remark that "it is not easy to judge a living artist on the yardstick of artistic greatness." He also managed to mention that a significant collection of this particular painter's work was in the very museum in which it always appeared that I had to drag him. He continued to speak eloquently about the artwork until the cab showed up. In fact, his spin was so good it could have been mistaken for a focused docent tour. In the taxi I exchanged a knowing glance with Bob.

For whatever reason, since then we have never spoken about the restaurant incident. Bob made partner and gave up the excessive amount of time he was spending after work at the gym. Instead, for recreational activities we often go to various museum exhibit openings together. I have joked with him about docent work, telling him, "You could be a contender!" Using the language of law, he still responds in terms of a demurrer, but he tells me his next goal in life is to start an art collection.

Rage Against the Shower; a Story

For several years I didn't recognize my teenage daughter: she had changed so much that I felt she had been replaced by a shape shifter whose punk interests were confined to surf and garage influences. Her grades plunged, her hair spiked and she admonished me if I even mentioned that her shower handle had rusted shut from lack of use. Then one day she threw away her grimy hoodie, (yes, the one I bought her for $42 at Bloomindales). She took the ring out of her nose and removed the stud from her tongue. She had her tattoos removed; well, the most offensive ones anyway.

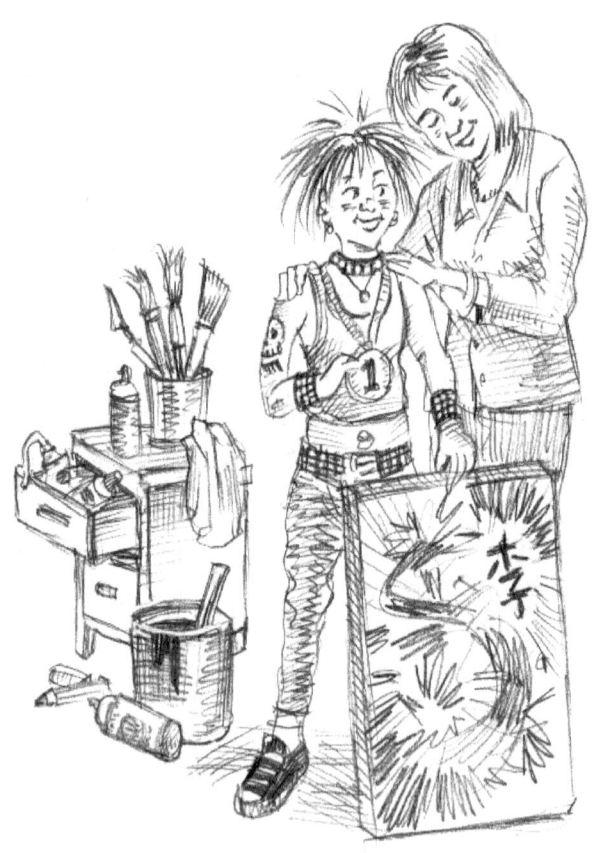

And to what did I owe this remarkable metamorphosis? It all started when she won first place in the city museum's prestigious high school art contest. Her artistic creations were displayed in the museum for all to see; public accolades abounded.

Since then she has remained a changed person. I could almost describe her as a whiz kid. Recently, she won an academic scholarship to an Ivy League university. I am fairly certain my daughter will continue to express her artistic talent and develop in the field of art. And I have almost as much confidence that she will use the shower in her new dorm room.

How do I thank the museum for recognizing my daughter's talents and instigating her transformation? There are no words!

The Family Zone and the Museum

"My husband and I always took our houseful of children to the museum's family art festivals. We enjoyed performances and puppet theaters and hands-on art activities.

"For a long time now, the children have been grown and gone: they are off to college or to work. But old habits die hard and my husband and I still go to the family programs at the museum. Maybe we just like to remember the good-old-days. Our fortunes are pinned on the hope that one day we will have grandkids to take to the museum's events. All these years the museum has been there for us and we have always been grateful."

Womankind Working For Mankind

A man comes into an art museum and while on tour he passes a statue of nude women, then winks, and nudges the

127

other men on the tour. (*Boom Boom*) This scenario is not a joke and the women are likely to be the first ones who see the unspoken double-standard and consequent baseness of the man's gesture. The point-of-view-from-the feminine could be seen as a form of elitism, but for hundreds of years the elite shoe was, collectively, on male feet. It was the lexicographer Samuel Johnson who, in the eighteenth century, explained what was for most people the general wisdom; that there are serious "rational" limitations when it comes to women's abilities. Johnson is quoted as saying, "Sir, a woman's preaching is like a dog's walking on his hind legs. It is not done well; but you are surprised to find it done at all."

From Aristophanes to I Love Lucy, women have been made fun of, and this is particularly true when it comes to the amount of talking that they do. Today, there is finally parity and nowhere is that more apparent than when women appear as art museum tour guides. In the case of art docents some of the esteem has to do with the setting; like real estate, it is location, location, location. Male and female docents alike are trained by museum education departments and are bound by museum rules. In this more gender neutral world for instance, there is no particular need to understand the territory covered by man games; the World Series it is not. What is necessary is to point out the artistic achievements on the walls. It goes without saying that female docent's explanations are elucidating art works that will fit into the wide-ranging legacy of people-kind. Perhaps because women can be loquacious, historically they have always excelled in this type of essential exploration of high culture.

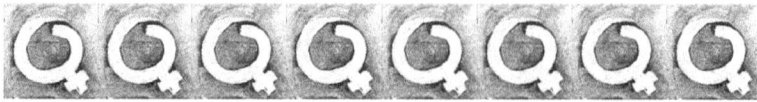

It is no Longer Cherchez la Femme

It is the twenty-first century and much has changed. Women have put away their crinolines and bloomers and their works and words are no longer lost in interpretation. Men, however, have lost their status as women's benevolent overlords.

Whether inside or outside the walls of the museum, women have bonded together: women artists of the twentieth and twenty-first century have, just like the Beatles song, "come together" and joined in camaraderie to create new visions. From the 1960's to today's postmodernism and beyond, women artists have found fresh ways to express their "herstories" which now grace the enclosures of American art museums.

Vocalizing to a Different Tune

As a woman tour guide, you have a voice which differs from the one used to call the family to dinner. The voice is different too, from a teacher's voice; there is more at stake. Standing in front of the remarkable museum art works, many of which are priceless masterpieces, marks the job of docent as different from a teacher standing in front of a blackboard. The docent position is defined in broad terms: there is a freedom that will allow you to create your own persona. Though the term "docent" in much of Europe refers to a person who is on a professorial rung of the academic ladder, in the United States, because a docent is usually a voluntary job, the duty is one of learned person…ebullient narrator…friendly moderator and knowledgeable guide. And because of the unambiguous proximity to known great works of art, the voice of both male and female docents is amplified.

Male Docents; A Valuable Commodity

Why are male docents highly valued? The list of their virtues is many and includes their rarity. It is sometimes easier to find your muse in an art museum than to find a male docent. This is not a secret only discovered by rifling through the files of J. Edgar Hoover: for whatever reason, there are far fewer men compared to women docents in an art museum. Because of this, when a male is trained and becomes a skilled docent, he stands out like a polished diamond among common stones.

Below is a candid, self-reflective conversation with a seasoned male docent about his role.

A conversation with Scott O'Connor, Docent at the Crocker Art Museum, Sacramento, California:

When I was asked what it is like to be a male docent in an art museum, I was perplexed. Compared to what? It seemed politically incorrect to even consider the question. However, upon further reflection it dawned on me I had many interesting experiences as a docent and some of these experiences were unique to being a male docent.

Why did you become a docent?

I became a docent not because I know a great deal about art and art history but because I don't. As an educator, I saw how students were transformed when involved in the arts and I wanted to explore why this is so.

Are there other reasons you became a docent?

I enjoy the company of strong-minded, intelligent, creative, well-read women. What better place to find them than an art museum?

I was also looking for a community of people with similar interests and involvement in the arts.

What is different about being a male in an art museum?

I discovered that there are differences – some substantial, some superficial, some silly.

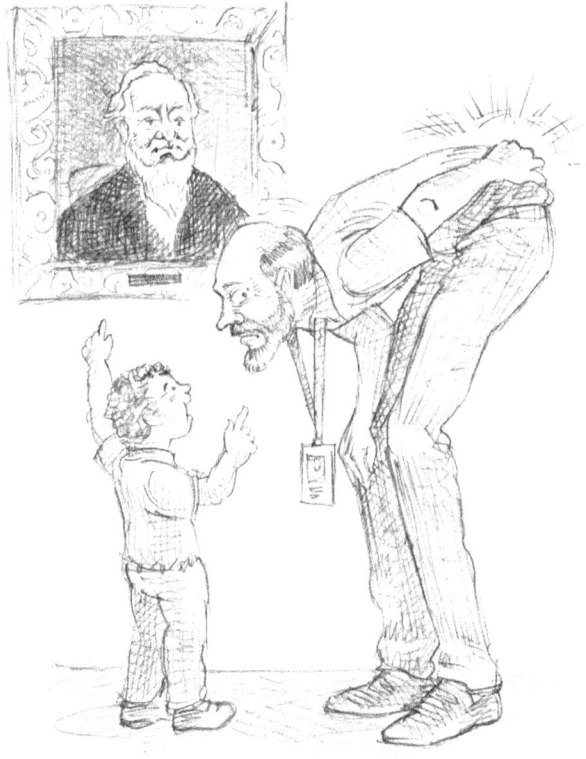

I am six feet tall, bald, with a beard. It is very easy to spot me in the museum. I tell young students that, if they ever

131

get lost, just look for the tall bald guy. The disadvantage is that at six feet tall, I am about a foot and a half taller than most third graders which makes it hard for me to hear their responses.

Another disadvantage is that when I give tours to children, I am sometimes mistaken for Judge Edwin Crocker (benefactor and namesake of the Crocker Art Museum where I am a docent). Judge Crocker has been dead for 140 years.

Nevertheless, I usually answer, "Yes."

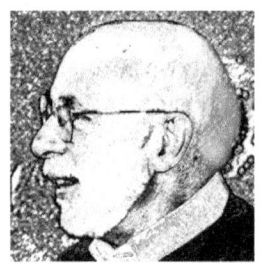

What are some of the "silly" aspects you mentioned?

Male docents seem to have instant name recognition among other docents and staff: I have my own nickname, "Rooster," given to me by the head of security. For reasons of companionship, identity, and security, we men refer to ourselves as "the tribe."

An advantage I have as a male docent is that I never have to wait in line for the restroom.

Are your assignments any different from the women docents?

I tend to get assigned to lead student groups that are junior high or high school-aged or groups that have the appearance of being a bit unruly.

Also, as an experienced docent, I am assigned to mentor "newbies:" docents who are still in-training. For some reason, men mentor men and women mentor women, though I am not sure why.

Do men have a unique identity in an art museum?

I don't think so, at least not as viewed by staff or other docents. The difference lies in serving as a role model for students. I think it is important and gratifying for students to see a male in a role primarily identified with women.

Do your techniques in touring differ in any way from women's?

No, we all learn the same skills and touring strategies; these are to observe, pose open-ended questions, reflect, share thoughts with colleagues and explore what new ideas might reveal themselves. The primary goal for all docents is to engage the group and not just entertain.

What has most surprised you about being a docent?

The docent training I received and my touring experiences have changed the way I think. I used to think of myself as a rational, linear, logical, organized thinker looking for the "right" answer. Colleagues sometimes called me anal-retentive which I took as an accurate description and a compliment! Now I take more time to observe, question, reflect, process, and consider the way I think. I'm more interested in the visual language of art – metaphor, iconography, color, technique, and symbol – and what they communicate. I have come to embrace and enjoy multiple interpretations of art. I now view the world as a more diverse, complex, layered, interesting place.

Staff, Crew and You

Because of its voluntary nature, you can always think of docent life as a second career, but never as a family business. This is to say, monetary remuneration will not be forthcoming. In some sense this immediately puts you at odds with the salaried employees at the museum: they are a group of educated professionals who have graduated in museum and art related studies and taken up the career as their livelihood. It is a basic problem, on the one hand the docent is a necessary and welcome part of the museum team; on the other hand the docent is a volunteer, an unpaid member of the museum who is usually not professionally trained in museology or art, and who can, at the drop of a hat, resign. Because of this freedom, on rare occasions the docent can freely become a nuisance to the staff.

Life in the Docent Trenches

There are ways in which, if only subliminally, the authority wielded by the museum professionals can irritate a volunteer. There are times when the question of acquiescence might enter a volunteer's head: just how compliant must a docent be? These thoughts, while not limited to volunteers, might surface more frequently in the mind of a person who is not being financially compensated and whether correctly or not, feels slighted by the staff.

This is the time to pull out one's grievances and, like shaking out questionable underwear, think about whether it is really necessary to air them in public.

Entrenched Power or Superior Work Ethic?

In judging your complaint, try for a sober, moderate and longer view of the situation, in this way a more temperate conclusion might predominate. It is helpful if hierarchy is understood. In the case of museum staff, the hierarchy is almost always won through a system of meritocracy. Since professional promotion in art museums does not come easily, most people who have positions of authority have struggled and worked hard to gain their level of standing. Generally their pedigrees are above suspicion and their achievements are to be respected and applauded. Though there might come a time when docents might feel that they have been asked to do something they consider unreasonable, when the situation is looked at through impartial lenses, it might be that their complaint does not quite rise to the level of a human rights violation.

It is true that there may be rare cases when there is a museum staff member who assumes that behind every problem there is a docent. But because volunteer tour guides are so highly valued, generally if there is a sticky exchange between a grumpy staff member and a docent, it might be because: 1) the museum staff members work tirelessly and are therefore, tired; or 2) because most museum employees, as compared to their equivalents in corporate America, are grossly underpaid; or 3) both.

A Recipe for Crazy

There is one situation which leads to difficulty that can be traced directly to the volunteer docent: it is very easy to become over-scheduled. If you promise you will do too much, there is a good chance you will do too little. Accepting too large a work load and then not following through, fans the flames of false hopes in the museum staff members who are counting on you. A good idea is to count to ten before agreeing in the affirmative to any of the following: a third marriage with a restrictive prenuptial; another refinance modification on your mortgage; a call for extra hours of volunteer work at the museum. Like the teenager at a free-for-all-party who has promised to remain intact, the word "no" should be part of a volunteer's vocabulary.

Adaptable for the Inevitable

An accommodating attitude contributes to general sanity. In any workplace that isn't controlled by leadership, disharmony and chaos can erupt that will demoralize staff and volunteers alike. This kind of environment will diminish creativity, productivity and accountability. As a volunteer docent, this is not the legacy and contribution you are striving for. Someone has to be in charge; in your heart of hearts aren't you glad it's not you?

In the end, the staff is permanent, but so are many of the docents. This acknowledgement can, at the very least, become the basis of a détente. Mutual respect is like dealing with relatives: it is melded in the fires of reality.

Artful Activities

There are many kinds of activities that a person is privy to once they are an inside player within the museum's tent. The privileges are so varied and sprinkled with so many one-of-a-kind experiences that no list could adequately cover the opportunities.

Here is a brief account of artful activities in which you can participate:

Artist's talks
Various instructive seminars
Art receptions
Travels to different museums
Travels to art studios
Book signings
Luncheons with like-minded guides and museum members
Exclusive museum dinner receptions
Mini-art classes
Shadowing of curators, museum directors and senior docents
Exclusive talks about special exhibits and traveling exhibits
Meeting and giving tours to visiting dignitaries
Foreign travel with museum docents and museum members
Informative colloquiums/workshops
School visits
Parties set up for the benefit of you, the museum tour guide

Interpersonal with the Inter-Cultural

The cure for many maladies such as loneliness and lack of stimulating conversation is to become involved in an environment that is brimming with edifying and enjoyable company. The art museum surroundings provide a springboard for social interaction that inspires and uplifts. It is a person-friendly place which constantly influences one's social life.

The dynamic relationships made in this swirling, ever-changing, wholesome soup bring new tastes and flavors that simmer for a lifetime. If you are seeking a network of new friends who have the right ingredients, try looking in the museum cookbook; it might just be the whole enchilada you were searching for.

In the Next Chapter...

The world of tour guides in Europe will be explored; their different situations might give you pause for thought. I hope your pause will be only temporary because in this last chapter we will be going the extra mile.

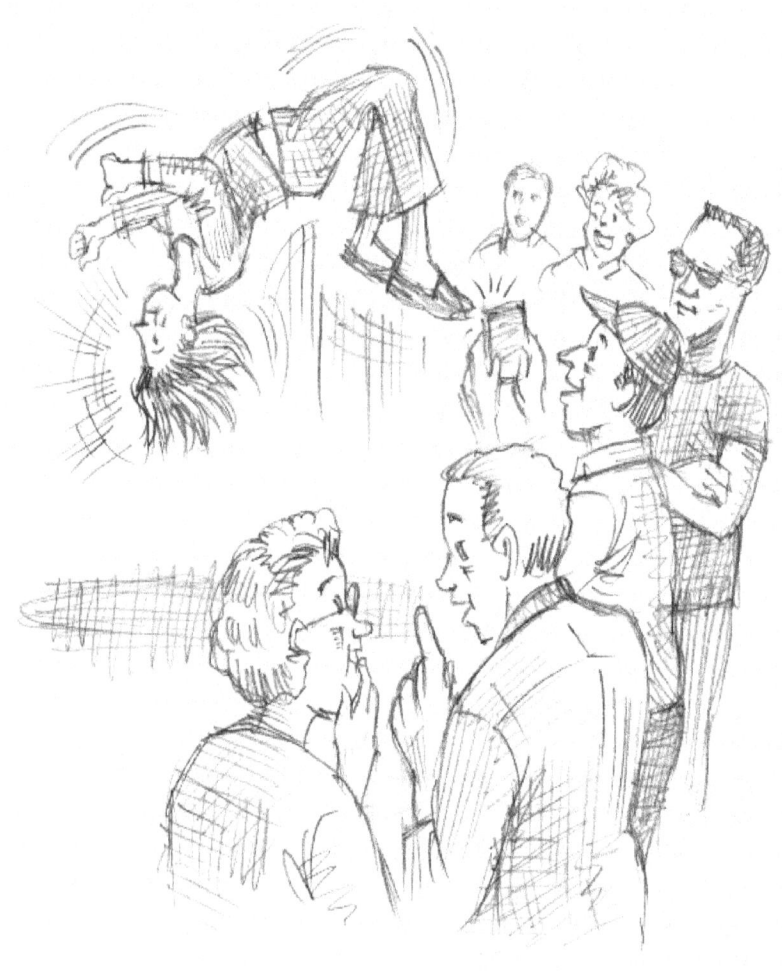

Docent Edith....Going the extra mile

Chapter Eight

"Art is enough for a lifetime, but a lifetime is not enough for art."   *Arthur Rubenstein*

Tour Guides in Europe/ Going the Extra Mile

Throughout this book, the term "docent" has been used interchangeably with the term "tour guide." But the meanings are much more refined in Europe; as an identifying title, "museum docent" does not exist. The Europeans take the term *docent* from the Latin word *docens*: a teacher. The docent in much of Europe is a specific educational rank within academia which is below *professor ordinaries* (professor). The best interpretation of the European meaning of *docent* is what American universities call a lecturer. Since a docent is an academic appointment attached to a college or university, it is a paid position. So the docent, in the continental meaning of the word, is not the person who leads you on a tour through an art museum.

Yet there are equivalent docent roles in European art museums. The function is the same; the customary term is "tour guide." When I was in Europe interviewing the tour guides in some of the larger art museums, I was met with blank stares when I told them the book I was writing about their activities was called *Docent Details.* For a European audience, the title would have to be *Tour Guide Details.*

Rule Britannia

Like the rest of Europe, the British call their docents, "tour guides." But to show their independent spirit, not only have the Brits not adopted the Euro, they also have tour guide standards which differ considerably from the rest of Europe. There is a headline which ran in an English newspaper that makes the British position quite clear: "Dense fog in the English Channel/ Europe Isolated"

Something that is similar in the British and American models is that the tour guides associated with the larger art museums (called galleries) are volunteers.

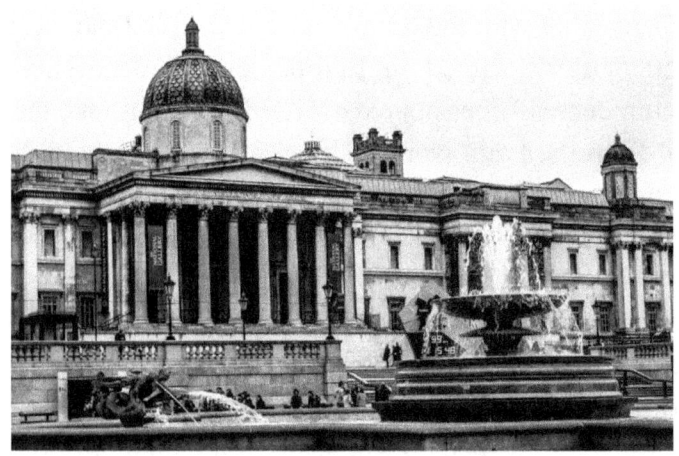

London's National Gallery

Alive, Alert and Adult

Each day at opening time there are long queues waiting to get into the London galleries. Entry is free. Free, too, are the public tours; this being somewhat of a rarity for European museums.

In Britain the organized tours are geared to adults. This is true in the National Gallery, the National Portrait Gallery, Tate Britain and even in the private Wallace collection.

In the great London art galleries, the tour guides focus on the historical and aesthetic aspects of the collections. In Tate Britain, for instance, the tour guides start with a short history of the sugar cube, since Mr. Tate made his money refining sugar and then wrapping it into little squares so that the English could have a convenient way to sweeten their tea and coffee.

In the vast halls that hold the thousands of artworks in the National Gallery the docents give general, introductory tours of five or six artworks, choosing no more than one work per gallery. Generally, the tours are 45 minutes to 1 hour 15 minutes long and quite refreshingly, are usually "spot on," as the Brits would say, not going over their stated time limit. There is an emphasis on spending a long duration of time at each stop: audience participation depends on the tour guide. Some guides ask that questions be held to the end, some tour guides ask for questions at each stop and some guides do not ask for any audience participation but, if queried, will answer questions along the way.

Keep Calm and Carry On

There are thousands of excited children's groups which spill out over the British art museum floors each month. Though they are not given official museum tours, their teachers and private guides perform this duty. It is easy to spot the enthusiastic students, many in uniform, sitting and standing, clutching their pencils or pieces of chalk and dutifully drawing on a piece of paper. "Copy and interpret the art," seems to be a well known phrase for these lively young apprentices.

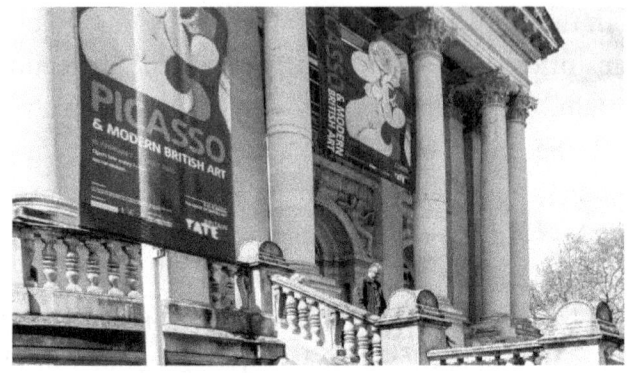

The Tate Britain

Vive la Difference!

The French system for tour guide qualifications and standards stand as an exemplar for much of Europe. A person wanting to become a tour guide must attend a three to four year program at a qualifying academic academy such as The School of the Louvre. The guide is given rigorous studies in historical, academic and aesthetic art theories. At the end of their studies, the students take qualifying examinations and are also interviewed by the officials at the Ministry of Culture. Just who will qualify for an official guide position has to do with a complex system of testing and scoring. In this hierarchy, it is the Ministry of Culture that makes the final selection as to which matriculated students will be hired for the national museums of France. The students must be competent to give tours in any of the national museums such as the Louvre, Versailles, Musee D'Orsay, L'Orangerie, etc. The encyclopedic knowledge that is required of a tour guide and the official imprimatur means that the position is looked upon as a profession, is highly sought after, and is paid well by the government. It is not the number of tours that the tour guide gives per week that ensures his/her pay. Instead, the tour guide's government income is assured as a monthly salary.

In the French system, students who are not hired for the national museums can become contract guides, working for the various agencies that specialize in tour groups.

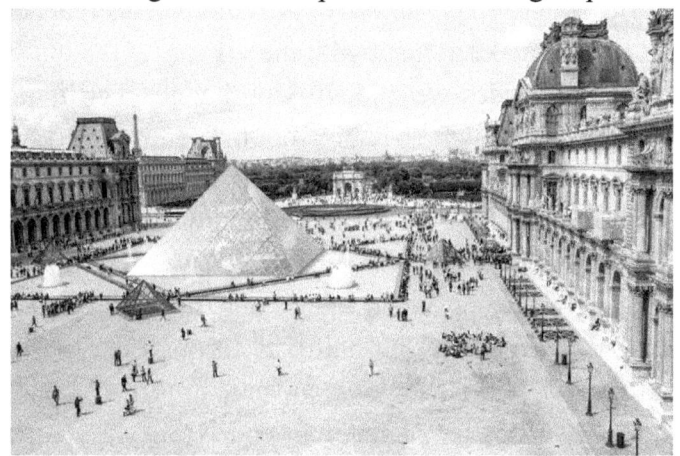

The Louvre, Paris

No Need to Scatter a Bread Crumb Trail

Inside the French national art museums, the attendance is jam-packed. At art stops such as the Mona Lisa, the hundreds of constantly cycling visitors feels like a forever-loop, making the experience of seeing the masterpiece a little like participating in a polite brawl.

Artists with their easels and art equipment are a common sight in the French art galleries. Would-be artists as well as superb copyists, all with their set-ups, can be seen in front of master works, carefully apply pigment to their canvasses and blithely ignoring the bottlenecks they are creating.

There is a paid admission policy for the French art galleries. There are also fees attached to museum tours.

Bravo at the Prado

There are some European museums such as the Prado in Madrid where the majority of guides are independent contractors and make contact with the visitors at the museum's entrance. The guides wear identifying badges, certifying that they have been through special schooling and are licensed to give tours. Cost of the tour is discussed with the potential tour-customer and when price and duration are agreed upon, the group or individual is off with their guide.

I originally consented to an hour tour at the Prado and my guide was excellent, but half way through the tour it was obvious that at her meticulous and attentive pace, one hour would not be sufficient. As the hour ended and she stopped the tour, it was easy to perceive that she was used to renegotiating her cost for the remainder of the tour. Though the activity of pulling out a wallet and exchanging money in front of a master work by Goya seemed more fitting for a scene at the local bazaar, the extra cost was well worth the price of the tour.

The Universal Museum/Then and Now

The original museum was called a *musaeum* and was a place where the ancients could get together and share substantive intellectual thoughts. It is possible to find the muses at a modern museum, but the contemporary muses are the new democratized models. The ancient muses seemed to serve a more limited audience, presiding over the loftier denizens of Greece such as the philosophers and scholars.

Repositories of Music and Poetry: But Where's the Art?

Musaeums did not have art collections in the contemporary sense of the meaning of the word. There was not a painting, not a poster, not a print, nor a piece of wall art in sight. Try to picture Archimedes, sitting in the *musaeum's* bathtub, discovering the principle of surface to volume ratio while carrying on an engaging conversation with his cohorts, and you get the idea. It was a place where (metaphorically) a Nobel Prize winner could discuss grand theories with an unkempt, intellectual Bohemian. Many men lived inside its sheltering confines and if they became staff members of the *musaeum*, they were salaried and paid no taxes. Much like now, the *musaeum* fostered social learning, but it did so without the artistic effects we have today to surround and inspire. Nevertheless, all in all, the *musaeum* must have been a cool place to hang out.

The Past/Present/Future

The museums of today are luring visitors with buildings that look like giant saucers, musical instruments, or titanic ships. Even the nostalgic older museums have built and attached annexes which are newer than cell phones. Once the visitor is inside, the interiors come alive with high-maintenance collections and entertainment that provide everything from undulating electronic projections of cyber art to child-oriented play rooms. The evening events give a whole new meaning to "a night at the museum."

Still, today's museums have managed to keep the Renaissance pledge; preserving historic images and relics created by the artists of the past. From Renaissance times on, visual literacy was the primary reason for museums to exist. Though art museums have gone through a huge shift and now embrace a wide range of interests, for those concerned with visual history, there is still no better place to see the authentic representations of the past.

There Are Apples and There Are Oranges

Since art museums vary widely, there are ways to classify them which helps to make sense of their differences. You might think of what type of collection engages you, and then choose the museum in your area that most closely resembles your interests. Below are the categories* followed by some museum examples:

The Encyclopedia Museum: The Museum of Fine Arts, Boston; The Metropolitan Museum of Art, New York; The Art Institute of Chicago

The Public Museum: National Gallery of Art; National Portrait Gallery

The Sculpture Museum: Nasher Sculpture Center, Dallas

The One-Artist Museum: Salvador Dali Museum, St. Petersburg, FL

The Garden/Park Museum: Frederik Meijer Gardens and Sculpture Park, Grand Rapids

The Residence Museum: The Getty Villa, Malibu; The Huntington Art Gallery, San Marino, CA

The Specialty Museum: MoMA, New York; Museum of Modern Art, San Francisco

The Academic Museum: Harvard Art Museums

*(Loosely adapted from Schjeldahl's classifications)

Example of an Encyclopedia Museum:

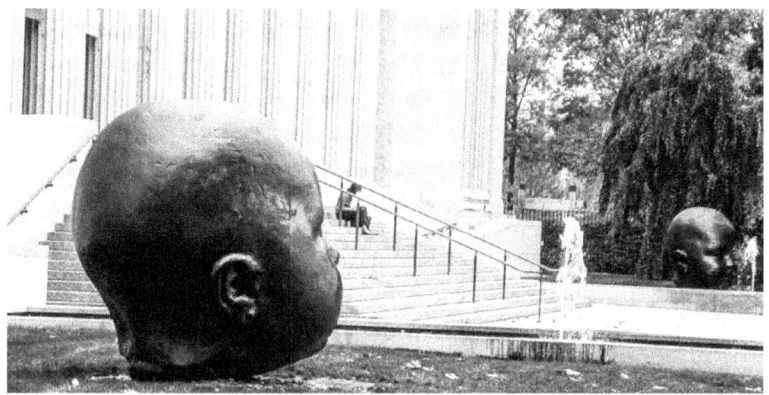

The Museum of Fine Arts, Boston

Getting Involved/Should You Go The Extra Mile?

Museums have countless pieces of art. The top museums in the United States have such an amazing number of artworks that they only exhibit approximately ten to fifteen percent of their collections. For a new visitor, it is like visiting the Land of Oz: for a single visit, they need to find a good wizard. It will be up to the tour guide to persuade the visitor that when the museum's sign says "open," it is just a manner of speaking and discreetly implies much more than one short visit.

If this book has convinced you of anything, it should have demonstrated that an art museum docent is a vital and invaluable link between the museum guest and the museum itself.

Many years ago, I was surprised to hear this very thought coming from an unlikely source. I attended a luncheon for Bay Area docents where Dianne Feinstein was the guest speaker. Although she became a U.S. senator, at the time she was mayor of San Francisco. Finestein talked in terms of how necessary an art docent's role is within the museum milieu and said that if she hadn't gone into politics, she would have chosen to become a docent.

Actively Serving with Determination

Serving is a refined practice. To serve is to approach any situation as a chance to give rather than expecting to receive. When you show up with focus and integrity and volunteer to give those inexhaustively various tours, you uncover the essential determination in your character.

You are also helping to craft the museum's destiny by persuading the visitors how luxurious and important it is to be physically present in the museum and how meaningful the museum is.

The Museum is where the Heart is

Once you decide on the museum of your choice, you will grow to love it and all it contains; its cycle of constantly changing exhibits, its funky art pieces hidden in corners, its all-star pieces that bring the museum fame. When you volunteer your time and effort at that museum, you cannot help but become invested in it. Jerry Seinfeld, when speaking of baseball teams, put it this way: "You root for the shirt." When you hear a docent from another museum talk about the superior place they work at, you realize that their heart belongs to a museum someplace else. Which is best? There is one museum here and there is another museum there: it is like judging an argument between two friends; it doesn't pay to think about reaching a decision.

Confidentiality Disclosed

There is no secret to becoming and sticking with docent work: one just stays informed and works to the best of one's ability. Along the way there is joy and satisfaction and frustration and instruction and inevitably, if one is holding on, the ride of a lifetime.

Looking Toward the Future through the Windshield of the Present

It is impossible to tell what changes will occur in the museums of today as they morph at warp speed into the museums of tomorrow. Where do you think you will be in the foreseeable future? If you choose to go the extra mile, it could be at the museum.

Afterword

For the last several years writing this book was my great problem to solve. It has taken up much of my life and has been my recreational activity, my hobby, and now my product. The contents were not written to disclose "the truth, the light and the way." I am sure there is a technique that would have winnowed down the pertinent information into summary form. Like Blaise Pascal, "I am sending you a long letter because I don't have time to write you a short one."

It is also clear that this book is by a docent, for people who would be or are docents. What is covered is an attempt to discuss the prosaic and commonplace. I hope I have given sufficient examples to show that there are many moving parts to becoming a docent in an art museum.

I'd love to hear from you. Let's have a conversation. Please contact me at my website: **www.docentinfo.com** *or email me at* **docentdetails@gmail.com**

For Groups/Clubs/Organizations: To schedule a PowerPoint talk on the topics discussed in <u>Docent Details,</u> please contact me at *docentdetails@gmail.com*

Index

Fluxus, 107

Preparation, 63
Public speaking, 68

R

Rap lyrics, 96
Renaissance, 17, 63, 91, 148

S

San Francisco Museum of Modern Art, 5, 103
Senior citizen, 78, 80
Smithson, James, 20
Stone Age, 12, 13

T

The Museum of Fine Arts, Boston, 148, 149
The Signature Exercise, 48
The Tate Britain, 144
Tour, 5, 59, 66, 85, 86, 112, 141

U

United Kingdom, 25

V

Visual Thinking Strategies, 34

W

Wall labels, 65
Whitney Museum of American Art, 24

www.ingramcontent.com/pod-product-compliance
Lightning Source LLC
Chambersburg PA
CBHW060852170526
45158CB00001B/328